Also by Jackie Silberg are these books available from
Gryphon House:

Games to Play With Babies
Games to Play With Toddlers

Games to Play with Two Year Olds

By Jackie Silberg

Illustrations by Linda Greigg

gryphon house

Beltsville, Maryland

Cover Design: Graves Fowler Associates
Cover Photo: Straight Shots

Published by Gryphon House, Inc., 10726 Tucker Street,
Beltsville, MD 20705

World Wide Web: http://www.ghbooks.com

Printed in the United States of America.

The author of this book, Jackie Silberg, is an acclaimed speaker, teacher
and trainer on early childhood development and music. You can arrange
to have her speak, present, train or entertain by contacting her through
Gryphon House, PO Box 207, Beltsville MD 20704-0207.

Liabrary of Congress Cataloging-in-Publication Data

Silberg, Jackie, 1934-
    Games to play with two year olds / Jackie Silberg ; illustrations by
Linda Greigg.
        p.   c.m.
    Include index.
    ISBN 0-87659-169-1 : $14.95

    1.Games. 2. Early childhood education. 3. Motor ability in
children. I. Title

GV1203.S538   1994   94-15716
790.1'922—dc2O   CIP

Table of Contents

Language Games

Young twos

Middle twos

Older twos

Running and Jumping Games

Animal Games

Older twos

Car Games

Young twos

Middle twos

Older twos

Art Games

Young twos

Middle twos

Counting Games

Teddy Bear Games

Imagination Games

Nursery Rhyme Games

Singing Games

Cooking Games

Nature Games

Quiet Games

From the Author

When I was a new mother celebrating the joys of parenting, I remember many of my friends with older children telling me about the "terrible twos" and how my child would change into a "monster."

When my son turned two, I was expecting all kinds of negative behavior and instead found a delightful, curious, interesting, precious and adorable two year old with a "joie de vivre."

Was my son different? Not one bit!! The myth prevails but the real truth is that two year old children are a joy and wonder. "No," "I can't" and "I want to do it myself" need love and support as your two year old struggles for independence.

This book is divided into chapters about daily subjects that interest your two year old. All the games are based on developmentally appropriate guidelines from the National Association for the Education of Young Children as well as Piagetian theory.

Permitting your child to take initiative and to be assertive is one of the greatest gifts that you can give him or her.

How lucky you are to have a two year old!!

Jackie Silberg

Guidelines for Growth

Motor, Auditory and Visual Skills

Likes to listen to the same story over and over

Develops enough hand-eye coordination to copy a line

Hops on one foot

Walks up and down stairs placing one foot on each stair

Runs freely

Uses scissors with one hand to cut paper

Jumps through a plastic hoop

Slides down a slide

Older twos can ride a tricycle

Jumps and lands with feet apart or with one foot in front of the other

Marches

Balances on a beam

Develops right or left handedness

Jumps from various heights

Follows simple directions

Matches six basic colors

Responds to music and rhythm by swaying and bending knees

Language and Cognitive Skills

Talks to self and to dolls

Understands and stays away from common dangers

Repeats part of a nursery rhyme or joins in

Understands the concept of one

Takes things apart for the purpose of learning

Groups things together by color, form or size

Uses short sentences to convey simple ideas

Takes apart and puts things together purposefully

Understands in, out and under

Knows that different activities happen at different times of the day

Expresses feelings, desires and problems verbally

Remembers and names objects absent for a short time

Identifies objects by their use

Is developing a vivid imagination

Beginning to use pronouns

Constantly asks the names of objects

Uses plurals of words

Self-Concept Skills

Finds own play area of activity

Likes to help parents around the house

Puts on own coat and shoes (can't tie or button)

Feeds self using a fork and spoon and glass.

Values playmates and friends

Feeds himself or herself

Drinks from a cup

Locates and names body parts

Sings part of a song

Brushes teeth

Puts together more complex puzzles

Likes talking on the phone

Enjoys going on excursions with an adult

Gives full name when asked

Refers to self by name

Gets drink without help

Shows pride in clothing

Helps put things away

Starts make believe play

Enjoys naming possessions of other, telling to whom they belong

Language Games

Look What I See!

♦ Put two chairs, or sit with your child in your lap, in front of a window in your house.

♦ Begin a conversation about what you see through the window. Ask your child, "What do you see in the yard?"

♦ Whatever the answer is, respond to it with another question. For example: if your child says, "Car," ask, "Where is the car going?"

♦ Try constantly to encourage your child to talk.

♦ Find magazines with pictures of what you saw through the window.

♦ Show the pictures to your child and remind her of what you talked about earlier.

 What your two year old will learn:
LANGUAGE SKILLS

Jack-in-the-Box

◆ Fingerplay rhymes give wonderful practice in language and use both sides of the brain.

◆ Say the following rhyme and do the actions:

> *Jack-in-the-box,*
>   *(make a fist by putting your thumb inside your fingers)*
> *Sit so still.*
> *Why don't you come out?*
> *I think I will.*
>   *(pull your thumb out from under your fingers and*
>   *make a popping sound with your mouth)*

 What your two year old will learn:
LANGUAGE SKILLS

The Cobbler

◆ Shoes and feet are fascinating to a two year old. They enjoy taking their shoes off and on.

◆ Play a cobbler game with your child.

◆ Tell him that you are a cobbler who is going to fix his shoe. Hold the shoe in your hand and say, "Bang and a bang and a bang, bang, bang."

◆ As you say these words, pretend to hammer on the shoe.

◆ Then say, "All fixed! You can wear it now."

◆ Ask your child to fix your shoe. As he hammers, say the same words, "Bang and a bang and a bang, bang, bang."

◆ Hold your child in your lap while saying the following rhyme:

> *There's a cobbler down our street*
> *Mending shoes for little feet.*
> *With a bang and a bang and a bang, bang, bang.*
>   *(tap his shoe as you say these words)*
> *Mending shoes the whole day long,*
> *Mending shoes to make them strong,*
> *With a bang and a bang and a bang, bang, bang.*
>   *(tap his shoe again)*

 What your two year old will learn:
CREATIVITY

C-C-C-C-Cold

Save this game for a cold day.

◆ Go outside with your two year old to feel the cold air. Say to him, "I'm c-c-c-c-cold." Encourage him to imitate you.

◆ Recite the following poem and let him join in on every other line:

> *There was a _____ (child's name) and he did sing,*
> *C-C-C-C-C-C-cold.*
> *Across the street the sound would ring,*
> *C-C-C-C-C-C-cold.*
> *No matter what he tried to say,*
> *C-C-C-C-C-C-cold.*
> *His words kept coming out this way,*
> *C-C-C-C-C-C-cold!*

◆ Repeat the poem and show your child how to put his arms across his chest as if he were shivering.

 What your two year old will learn:
IMITATION

Touching Trip

◆ Two year olds love to touch things. You can help your child become more aware of what she is touching by calling attention to it.

◆ Bath time is a good time to talk about how toenails feel hard and hair feels silky.

◆ Take a touching trip through your house. To make it fun, say this little poem and then touch the object.

> *Touching time, touching time,*
> *Now it's time to touch the _____. (Name the object)*

◆ Pick out different textures: soft, hard, cold, slippery, rough, prickly, etc.

◆ Make comparisons with your child. "This feels hard and this feels soft."

What your two year old will learn:
ABOUT TEXTURES

Who's at the Door?

◆ Play a knock-at-the-door game with your two year old.

◆ Either you or your child should go into another room and close the door.

◆ Then you knock on the door. Your child says, "Come in. Who is it?" Then open up the door and say, "It's me."

◆ Now let your child do the knocking, and you say, "Come in, who is it?"

◆ Ask your child to pretend to be a dog. After you say, "Come in, who is it," he opens the door and barks like a dog.

 What your two year old will learn:
IMAGINATION

Show Me How You....

◆ This game helps your child follow directions by encouraging her to listen to what you say.

◆ Start each direction with "Show me how you...." and continue the sentence.

◆ This game can get silly. Your two year old will love it.

◆ As you give the direction, perform the action so that your child can imitate you.

> *Show me how you touch your head to your shoulder.*
> *Show me how you touch your ear to the chair.*
> *Show me how you touch Mommy on the nose.*
> *Show me how you touch your ankles.*
> *Show me how you touch Daddy on the neck.*

◆ Praise your child each time she performs an action correctly.

What your two year old will learn:
LISTENING SKILLS

Family Talk

◆ Gather pictures of family members.

◆ Show the pictures to your child and identify each picture with a single name: "Mommy, Daddy, Papa, Nanny," etc.

◆ Spread the pictures out on a table, and ask your child to find Mommy or Daddy, etc.

◆ Hold up a picture and say to your two year old, "Who is this?" Whatever her answer may be, repeat the correct answer.

◆ Look at the pictures again and say something about each person after they have been identified. For example: "Papa loves you very much" or "Nanny has a pretty smile."

◆ What your two year old will learn:
OBSERVATION SKILLS

Rain on the Green Grass

This rhyme can be a catalyst for language development.

◆ Say the following rhyme to your child:

> *Rain on the green grass,*
> *Rain on the sea,*
> *Rain on the housetops,*
> *But not on me!*

◆ When you come to the words "but not on me," put your hands on your hips and shake your head "no" vigorously.

◆ Substitute familiar words for the words in the poem. For example:

> *Rain on the table,*
> *Rain on the floor,*
> *Rain on the doggie,*
> *But not on me!*

◆ Soon your child will get the idea and will tell you what words to say.

◆ Always end with the same words "but not on me!"

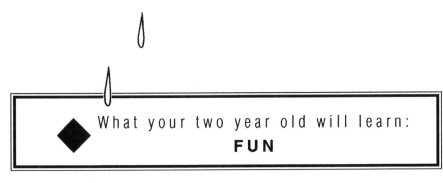

What your two year old will learn:
FUN

Is This the Choo Choo Train?

◆ Call and response poems are wonderful vehicles for developing language in your two year old.

◆ In the following poem, the child's response will always be the same two words: "Oh, yes."

◆ Even if your two year old isn't talking much, you will see how much he responds to this game.

◆ At first, say the words "Oh, yes" with your child.

> *Is this the choo choo train?*
> *Oh, yes.*
> *Does it chug along?*
> *Oh, yes.*
> *Choo, choo, choo,*
> *Oh, yes.*
> *Let's choo choo to the kitchen,*
> *Oh, yes.*
> *Let's choo choo to the door,*
> *Oh, yes.*

◆ Chug along like a train as you say the words and keep choo chooing until your child tires of the game.

◆ Two year olds really love to play this game.

 What your two year old will learn:
LANGUAGE SKILLS

No, No, No

◆ Two year olds love to assert themselves with the word "no." This game can turn a stressful situation into a more relaxed and humorous one.

◆ Shake your head "no" as you say the following rhyme:

> *No, no, no.*
> *I like to say, "no,*
> *No, no, no."*
> *I like to say, "no,*
> *No, no, no, no, no,*
> *No, no, no, no, no,*
> *No, no, no."*
> *I like to say, "no."*

◆ Your child will quickly join you in this little game.

◆ Show her how to shake her finger at the same time that she is saying, "no." Shake your head up and down and repeat the rhyme with the word "yes."

 What your two year old will learn:
SELF-EXPRESSION

Jack-a-Nory

◆ This familiar poem has wonderful possibilities for helping your two year old begin to form simple sentences.

◆ Say the rhyme.

> *I'll tell you a story*
> *About Jack-a-Nory,*
> *And now my story's begun.*
> *I'll tell you another*
> *About his brother,*
> *And now my story is done.*

◆ After your child has heard this poem a few times, change the words "Jack-a-Nory" to your child's name.

◆ After the line "and now my story's begun," add two simple sentences.

> *Once upon a time there was a little girl*
> *named _____ (child's name).*
> *She liked to play with toys.*

◆ Now finish the rhyme.

◆ Keep inserting two or three sentences after "and now my story's begun." Soon your child will be making up her own sentences.

 What your two year old will learn:
THINKING SKILLS

Rebus Stories

◆ A rebus is a picture that represents a word. The ancient Egyptians told stories using pictures this way. Your story should be two or three sentences long.

◆ Telling a story about what your two year old likes to do is the best way to begin.

◆ You can cut the rebus pictures from magazines, or you can draw them. Coloring books are also excellent sources for pictures.

◆ At the beginning, only use one picture.

◆ Identify the pictures and tell the story. For example, with a picture of a little boy, a dog and a swing, your story could be:

Once upon a time there was a little boy named _____ (child's name). He had a dog named _____ (dog's name). They went outside to play on the swing.

◆ Print out the words and read them to your child, touching each word as you say it.

◆ Rebus stories introduce children to the mechanics of reading, following the text from left to right and top to bottom.

 What your two year old will learn:
PRE-READING SKILLS

Bears Eat Honey

◆ Say the following rhyme with your child:

> *Bears eat honey,*
> *Cows eat corn,*
> *What do you eat when you get up in the*
> *   morn?*

◆ Talk about what you eat for breakfast.

◆ Repeat the rhyme starting with your child's name. Keep everything else the same.

> _____ *(child's name) eats toast,*
> *Cows eat corn, etc.*

◆ Talk about different animals and what they eat. Start the rhyme with a different first line and keep everything else the same.

> *Dogs eat bones....*
> *Rabbits eat carrots....*
> *Monkeys eat bananas....*
> *Babies eat oatmeal....*

◆ What your two year old will learn:
WORD ASSOCIATIONS

This Is the Father

◆ This is a very nice fingerplay that talks about the whole family.

◆ Hold up one finger at a time as you say the rhyme.

◆ On the last line, hold up all your fingers to represent "the family."

> *This is the father short and stout, (thumb)*
> *This is the mother with children about, (index finger)*
> *This is the brother tall you see, (middle finger)*
> *This is the sister with a toy on her knee, (ring finger)*
> *This is the baby sure to grow, (pinky)*
> *And here is the family all in a row. (all five fingers)*

◆ Count your fingers - 1, 2, 3, 4, 5.

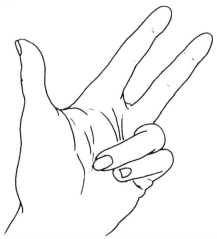

 What your two year old will learn:
COORDINATION

Taking Trips

◆ Taking your two year old to a variety of places will develop her vocabulary.

◆ Each time you go to a different place, you can talk about it before and after.

◆ You can draw pictures about what you saw on your trip and find books about the place that you visited.

◆ A few suggested places are: the fire station, the police station, the airport, the train station, an apple orchard, a farm, the zoo, etc.

◆ Hang a bulletin board or a large chart on a wall in your child's room. Each time you visit a new place, put a picture of that place on the chart. This will give you a chance to recall with your child where you visited.

 What your two year old will learn:
CREATIVITY

Telephone Fun

◆ Two year olds love to talk on the telephone, whether it's a real telephone or a pretend one.

◆ Get two play telephones, one for you and one for your two year old.

◆ Make up pretend conversations.

◆ When you begin, ask questions that only require a one word answer.

> *Adult: Hello.*
> *Child: Hello.*
> *Adult: Where is your hair?*
> *Child: Here. (she can answer or point to her hair)*

◆ Keep making up questions that require an answer. This develops your child's vocabulary.

◆ Another nice telephone game is to pretend to call people that your child knows. You make the call, and let your child be daddy, grandma, the dog, etc. This will help your child think about answering the questions in different ways.

◆ Always end each conversation with "Goodbye."

 What your two year old will learn:
CREATIVITY

The Thimble Family

◆ Using magic markers, paint faces on plastic thimbles.

◆ The faces can represent members of the family: Mom, Dad, pets, etc.

◆ Put a thimble on your finger and give another one to your child. Make up a conversation based on the thimble you are wearing.

◆ Ask questions that require a simple answer, for example, "Where are you going today?"

◆ Show your child how to move her finger all around as she talks for the thimble.

◆ Try changing voices for different thimble characters.

 What your two year old will learn:
IMAGINATION

Puppet Talk

◆ Get a puppet with hands. The kind that allows you to use your thumb, index and middle fingers is a good choice.

◆ Show your two year old all the different things that the puppet can do with its hands: clap, wave and pat. Show your child what the puppet can do with its head: nod, shake yes and shake no.

◆ Sing this song to the tune of "Mary Had a Little Lamb." When you sing the puppet's part, raise or lower your voice.

> *Puppet, can you clap your hands,*
> *Clap your hands, clap your hands?*
> *Puppet, can you clap your hands,*
> *Clap your hands today?*
>
> *(In the puppet voice)*
> *Yes, I can clap my hands,*
> *Clap my hands, clap my hands.*
> *Yes, I can clap my hands,*
> *Clap my hands today. (make puppet clap its hands)*

◆ Continue singing more verses.

Puppet, can you wave your hands...., Puppet, can you shake your hands....,Puppet, can you nod your head....

 What your two year old will learn:
LISTENING SKILLS

I Spy

◆ You probably played this game when you were a child. This version is adapted for two year olds, and you will find that it really helps develop language.

◆ You will need a hollow tube to look through. If you want to use real binoculars, that would be an added dimension.

◆ Look through the binoculars and say:

> *"I spy with my little eye, something that is blue.*
> *Is it the chair? No, it's not the chair.*
> *Is it the floor? No, it's not the floor.*
> *Is it my shoe? Yes, it is my shoe."*

◆ Now let your child hold the binoculars and repeat the game.

◆ Encourage your child to say the words. After you say, "Is it the chair," ask your child to say, "No, it's not the chair."

◆ He will probably say, "no" immediately and, as the game progresses, add more words.

◆ This is a humorous game for two year olds. They love to look for things that they recognize. For example, if you are looking for a teddy bear and you say, "Is it the door? No, it's not the door," your child will probably find it hilarious.

 What your two year old will learn:
THINKING SKILLS

The Bear Hunt

This version is perfect for your two year old

◆ Tell your child to copy your actions and repeat your words, one line at a time.

◆ Sit on the floor facing your child. Start tapping your hands on the floor in a steady rhythm. Keep tapping as you say the words, unless you are performing another action.

Going on a bear hunt, going on a bear hunt,
I'm not scared. (point to yourself and shake your head "no")
Oh, look, (shade your eyes as if you see something far away)
Here's a lot of rocks, let's walk through. (stand up and pretend
*   to be walking barefoot on rocks as you say:)*
Ouch, ouch, ouch.
Oh, look, Here's some very tall grass, let's walk through.
*   (part the tall grass as you say:)*
Swish, swish, swish.
Here comes a river, uh oh, no bridge.
Let's swim across. (swim with your arms)
Here comes a big tree, let's climb to the top.
*   (move fist over fist)*
Oh, look, there's a great big cave.
*   (pretend to be looking through binoculars)*
Let's climb down the tree and look in the cave. (climb downwards)
Let's go in the cave. (speak in a very soft voice)
Oh, look, I see two yellow eyes. (speak in a very soft and scared
*   voice)*
Help, it's the bear! Run....
*   (retrace all of the actions back to the beginning)*
Phew! We're safe.

 What your two year old will learn:
IMITATION

Running and Jumping Games

Jumpity Jumpity

◆ Two year olds love to jump, and jumping with both feet at once takes practice.

◆ Start jumping with your child while holding both of her hands.

◆ When she seems to be jumping in a rhythmic movement, try holding only one of her hands.

◆ Jumping on a trampoline or a mattress makes this game easier.

◆ Show her how to bend her knees as she jumps.

◆ Say this rhyme while you jump.

> *Jumpity, jumpity, jump, jump,*
> *Up to the sky, way up high.*
> *Jumpity, jumpity, jump, jump,*
> *See me jumping now.*

◆ When you feel your child is ready, let go of her other hand and see if she can jump by herself.

 What your two year old will learn:
COORDINATION

Streamers

◆ Crepe paper streamers are excellent accompaniments for all kinds of running and movement.

◆ There are many things to do with streamers: twirl them, shake them, weave them in and out, run with them behind you.

◆ Play instrumental music for your two year old. The streamers will help him move to the music more easily.

◆ Play fast and slow music. Try some very fast and furious music.

◆ Streamers are wonderful to take outside and run with in the wind.

◆ Try holding a streamer in your hand and running in the wind. You will feel like you are flying.

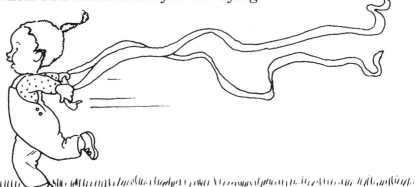

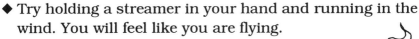

◆ **What your two year old will learn:**
COORDINATION

Andy Spandy

♦ This is a favorite movement game for two year olds. It is quick and action-oriented.

♦ Recite the poem and do the actions.

> *Andy Spandy, sugar candy, I pop down.*
> *Andy Spandy, sugar candy, I pop up.*
> *Andy Spandy, sugar candy, I pop in.*
> *Andy Spandy, sugar candy, I pop out.*

♦ This poem is very good for language development because the same words are repeated, encouraging your child to say them.

♦ Instead of using the word "pop," say hop, jump or any other word that occurs to you.

 What your two year old will learn:
COORDINATION

One, Two, Ready, Run

◆ Two year olds have so much energy. Running is one of their favorite activities.

◆ Play this game outdoors where you can run freely.

◆ Take three scarves of different colors and tie them to different objects like trees or a fence. Make sure each object is running distance from the others.

◆ Say to your child, "One, two, ready, run!" Run to the tree.

◆ When you have reached the tree, say, "One, two, now I'm done."

◆ Repeat the same word pattern as you run from one object to another.

◆ If your two year old is interested in colors, identify the scarf you are running towards by its color: "Let's run to the blue scarf."

 What your two year old will learn:
LISTENING SKILLS

My Feet

◆ Talk about feet with your two year old. Talk about all the different things that you can do with your feet.

◆ Recite the following poem and do the actions:

> *I can walk on my feet,*
> *Walk, walk, walk.*
> *I can hop on my feet,*
> *Hop, hop, hop.*
> *I can jump with my feet,*
> *Jump, jump, jump.*
> *Now sit down and rest.*
>
> *I can march with my feet,*
> *March, march, march.*
> *I can tiptoe on my feet,*
> *Tip, tiptoe.*
> *I can run with my feet,*
> *Run, run, run.*
> *Now sit down and rest.*

 What your two year old will learn:
LISTENING SKILLS

'Round and Stop

◆ Two year olds love to run and stop. This game gives them an opportunity to develop their motor and listening skills as they run around the room.

◆ Say "'round and 'round and 'round and stop!" As you say the words, walk around the room, and on the word "stop," sit down on a chair.

◆ Ask your two year old to join you in the game. You can hold his hand as you move around, or let him walk alone.

◆ Once he has the idea, try other movements: jumping, marching, hopping and crawling, for example.

◆ Your child will love the "stop" part!

 What your two year old will learn:
LISTENING SKILLS

Hopping Feet

◆ Running, jumping and hopping are probably the three favorite activities of a two year old.

◆ Show your two year old how to stand on one foot. Hold him as he tries to balance himself.

◆ While he stands on one foot, lift him up and down to show him what hopping means. Don't worry if he cannot do this alone. As he gets older and understands how to hop, he will do it when he is ready.

◆ Recite the poem and perform the actions.

Take your little foot and hop, hop, hop.
   (hop with one or both feet)
When you are tired, you can stop, stop, stop.
   (stop hopping)
Turn around and count to ten.
   (turn around and count to ten)
Take your foot and hop again.
   (start hopping)

 What your two year old will learn:
TO FOLLOW DIRECTIONS

Bouncy Bouncy

◆ Have you ever noticed how much your two year old loves to bounce on the bed or sofa? Make a game out of it.

◆ Hold your child's hand as she bounces up and down on the bed or sofa. As she bounces, chant:

> *Bouncy, bouncy, _____ (child's name)*
> *Bouncy, bouncy, _____ (child's name)*
> *Bouncy, bouncy, _____ (child's name)*
> *Bouncy, bouncy, boom!*

◆ On the word "boom," stop or fall down, whichever your child prefers.

◆ Invite a teddy bear or a stuffed animal to join you. Your child can hold the stuffed animal as you play the game. On the word "boom," she can drop the animal so that it goes "boom," too.

◆ Soon you will see your two year old playing this game with her stuffed animals.

What your two year old will learn:
BALANCE

The Pilot

◆ Ask your child to stretch her arms out to the side.

◆ Show her how to run around the room like an airplane, saying, "zoom."

◆ Tell your child, "Now it's time to come in for a landing." Show her how to move more slowly and finally land.

◆ Say this rhyme and perform the actions.

> *The pilot and plane fly all around the sky. (stretch out*
> *your arms and fly around the room)*
> *She zooms up high,*
> *(fly with your arms up high)*
> *She zooms down low,*
> *(fly with your arms low)*
> *And flies as fast as she can go.*
> *(fly around as fast as you can go)*
> *Landing time!*
> *(fall to the floor)*

What your two year old will learn:
IMAGINATION

Follow the Tape

◆ Make paths across the floor with masking tape. You can also do this outdoors.

◆ Make the path curve and turn and go a lot of different directions.

◆ Hold your child's hand and walk along the path with him. As you walk, sing the song, "Oh, Do You Know the Muffin Man?"

◆ When your two year old understands that he can walk on the masking tape and follow it, suggest that you travel the path in a different way.

◆ Try hopping, running, sliding, marching, walking backwards and tiptoeing.

◆ "The Muffin Man" is a big favorite of two year olds. You can also sing other favorite songs.

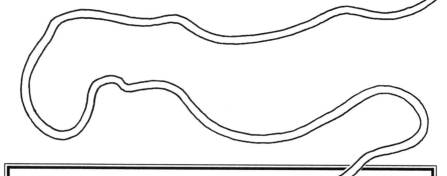

◆ What your two year old will learn:
BALANCE

The Movement Game

◆ Your two year old has amazing agility by now and can begin to use the movements he already knows in different ways.

◆ This game will also increase his vocabulary.

◆ Demonstrate all the following movements to your child, one at a time, and ask him to imitate you after each demonstration.

Take giant steps.
Walk backward.
Take tiny steps.
Walk sideways.
Jump fast.
March backward.

◆ What your two year old will learn:
TO FOLLOW DIRECTIONS

The Gingerbread Man

This is a good transition game

◆ Tell your own version of "The Gingerbread Man." A two year old's attention span is very short, so the story should be, too.

◆ Here is an idea:

> *Once upon a time there was a little ginger-bread man who loved to run. After breakfast he would say, "Run, run, as fast as you can. You can't catch me, I'm the gingerbread man."*

◆ Each time you say the words "run, run," take your child's hand and run in a circle.

◆ Continue the story, adding about two sentences at a time. For example:

> *The gingerbread man went to see his grandma, and when he got there he said, "Run, run, as fast as you can. You can't catch me, I'm the gingerbread man."*

◆ Soon your two year old will understand that whenever he hears "run, run," it's time for him to run.

◆ As a special treat, finish this game with a real ginger-bread man.

 What your two year old will learn:
LISTENING SKILLS

Visiting Aunt Sally

◆ Stand on the opposite side of the room facing your child.

◆ Say the following rhyme:

> *Billy Boy, Billy Boy,*
> *Come and see Aunt Sally.*
> *How will you come today?*
> *Come and see Aunt Sally.*

◆ Help your child decide how he will come to you. Here are some ideas: hop, jump, walk, run, walk backwards, walk sideways, crawl, like a rabbit, like a cat, etc.

◆ When he tells you what he is going to do, say, "Ready, set, Go!"

◆ When he reaches you, give him a big hug and say, "Time to go home." He goes back to the other side of the room, and you can play the game again.

◆ Change the words "Billy Boy" to your child's name.

 What your two year old will learn:
COORDINATION

Jump to the Wall

◆ This game is best played outside. Hold your child's hand and show him how to jump up and down.

◆ Say "One, two, jump to the wall."

◆ Hold your child's hand and jump to the nearest wall.

◆ As you are jumping, sing to the tune of "Frere Jacques":

> *We are jumping, we are jumping,*
> *Jump, jump, jump,*
> *Jump, jump, jump,*
> *Jumping, jumping, jumping,*
> *Jumping, jumping, jumping,*
> *Jump, jump, jump,*
> *Jump, jump, jump.*

◆ Pick out another place to jump to, for example, "One, two, jump to the fence."

◆ Keep playing the game, jumping to different places.

What your two year old will learn:
COORDINATION

Jumping Jacks

◆ Older twos enjoy jumping very much. Learning to do jumping jacks will develop their motor skills and balance.

◆ Show your two year old how to jump and land with her feet together. Do it yourself, then ask her to copy you.

◆ Jump and land with your feet apart. Again, do it first, then ask her to copy you.

◆ When she can jump both ways, show her how to alternate the two.

◆ As you do jumping jacks, say the following poem:

> *Jump one,*
> *Jump two,*
> *Look, look what _____ (child's name) can do.*
> *Feet together,*
> *Feet apart,*
> *This will exercise your heart.*

 What your two year old will learn:
COORDINATION

Hop Little Rabbit

◆ Recite the poem and perform the actions.

> *Hop little rabbit, hop, hop, hop. (hop around the room)*
> *Hop little rabbit, don't you stop. (keep hopping)*
> *Hop little rabbit, one, two, three. (keep hopping)*
> *Hop little rabbit, hop to me. (have your child hop to*
>   *you and then fall down together on the ground)*

◆ You can change the word "hop" to other motor skills—
jump, run, march, tiptoe, etc.

 What your two year old will learn:
COORDINATION

The Chair Game

◆ Tie a rope about two inches off the floor between two chairs.

◆ Ask your child to jump over the rope.

◆ When she can do that, ask her to step over the rope.

◆ Continue doing actions over and under the rope.

◆ Turn the game into a "Follow the Leader" game, with you as the leader. Here are some things that you can do.

> *Jump forward and jump backwards over the rope.*
> *Step forward and step backwards over the rope.*
> *Slide under the rope.*
> *Crawl under the rope.*
> *Run and jump over the rope.*
> *Hop to the rope and step over it.*

◆ As your child progresses, make the rope higher.

 What your two year old will learn:
COORDINATION

Hello Feet

◆ This rhythm poem is fun to do with your two year old. Be sure to stop as soon as you say, "Go to bed."

Hello feet, let's feel the beat. (tap your foot on the floor)
Hello knee, zip a dee dee. (bend your knees)
Hello thigh, my, oh, my. (move your leg back and forth)
Hello hip, pip, pip, pip. (move your hips back and forth)
Hello shoulder, get a little older.
*   (move your shoulders in a circular motion)*
Hello neck, pick, pick, peck.
*   (stretch your neck in the air)*
Hello head. (turn your head back and forth)
Go to bed! (pretend to go to sleep)

 What your two year old will learn:
BODY AWARENESS

Moving Around

◆ This rhyme gives your two year old a chance to run and jump and then quietly sit down.

◆ Say the rhyme and follow its directions.

> *Wiggle your fingers and clap your hands,*
> *Quickly turn around.*
> *Hop this way,*
> *Hop that way,*
> *Bend over and touch the ground.*
>
> *Wiggle your fingers and clap your hands,*
> *Quietly sit down.*
> *Bend this way,*
> *Bend that way,*
> *Don't make a sound, ssshhhhh.*

 What your two year old will learn:
TO FOLLOW DIRECTIONS

Animal Games

Pokey Snail

◆ This poem suggests many different ways to move.

◆ Say the poem and do the actions.

> *Pokey snail, pokey snail,*
> *You crawl so s...l...o...w.*
>> *(crawl very, very slowly on the floor)*
> *Hop toad, hop toad, this is how you go.*
>> *(hop around the floor like a toad)*
> *Noisy cricket, noisy cricket, why do you jump so high?*
>> *(jump around like a cricket)*
> *Only little birdies fly up in the sky.*
>> *(fly like a bird)*

 What your two year old will learn:
COORDINATION

Animal Moves

◆ Cut out pictures of animals from magazines. Select animals with which your child is familiar.

◆ Glue the pictures on separate sheets of construction paper.

◆ Show the animal cards to your child and discuss each one. Talk about what the animal says and how the animal moves.

◆ Demonstrate how the animal moves and let your child try to do it, too.

◆ Use exaggerated movements so that your two year old can better understand the size of the steps. For example, an elephant would take very slow, lumbering steps, and a kitty might take very quick and light steps.

◆ Put all the animal cards on a table. Ask your child to pick one card.

◆ Tell the name of the animal that she selected and ask her to move like that animal.

 What your two year old will learn:
COORDINATION

Here Is a Bunny

◆ Look at pictures of rabbits and bunnies with your child.

◆ Try hopping like a bunny and sniffing like a bunny.

◆ Pretend to be a bunny and eat a bunny lunch of carrots.

◆ Recite the following poem and perform the actions:

> *Here is a bunny with ears so funny.*
> *(hold up your pointer and middle finger)*
> *And here is his home in the ground.*
> *(cup your other hand)*
> *A noise he hears and he pricks up his ears,*
> *(move your two fingers that are standing up)*
> *And jumps to his home in the ground.*
> *(dive your fingers into your cupped hand)*

 What your two year old will learn:
COORDINATION

Animal, Wake Up

◆ Talk about the different animals that your child recognizes and the sounds that they make.

◆ Pretend that you and your child are bees. Make a buzzing sound and fly around the room.

◆ Now say that it is time for all the little bees to go to sleep.

◆ Close your eyes and pretend to be sleeping.

◆ Say to your child, "Wake up little bee." Take a deep breath in, then breathe out with a buzzing sound. Encourage your child to imitate you.

◆ Get up and buzz around the room again.

◆ Each time you play this game, make a different animal sound. The fun part will be taking a deep breath and exhaling with an animal sound.

What your two year old will learn:
THINKING SKILLS

At the Farm

◆ Your two year old loves to make animal sounds. She is very proud that she can make the different sounds.

◆ Look at picture books of animals, and ask your child to tell you what sounds the different animals make.

◆ Play this game with your child. You say the first three lines of this rhyme, and she makes the animal sound at the end of the fourth line.

> *Pigs at the farm go "oink, oink, oink,"*
> *Pigs at the farm go "oink, oink, oink,"*
> *Pigs at the farm go "oink, oink, oink,"*
> *The pigs go (Child says) "oink, oink, oink."*

◆ Continue repeating the rhyme and letting your child fill in the last line.

> *Dogs at the farm go "woof, woof, woof...."*
> *Cats at the farm go "meow, meow, meow...."*
> *Chickens at the farm go "cluck, cluck, cluck...."*
> *Frogs at the farm go "ribbit, ribbit, ribbit...."*
> *Bees at the farm go "buzz, buzz, buzz...."*

 What your two year old will learn:
ABOUT ANIMAL SOUNDS

What Does It Say?

◆ Place the animal cards from "Animal Moves" (page 61) in various locations throughout your house.

◆ Tell your child that you are going to look for animals. Hold his hand and start walking to the places where you have put the cards.

◆ As you are walking toward the card, say the following poem:

> *I see a _____ (name of animal), what does it say?*
> *What does it say?*
> *What does it say?*
> *I see a _____ (name of animal), what does it say?*
> *Tell me what does it say.*

◆ On the last line, "Tell me what does it say," pick up the card and make the animal sound.

 What your two year old will learn:
ABOUT ANIMAL SOUNDS

Happy Little Cat

◆ Your two year old loves to make animal sounds.

◆ Read a book about farm animals and practice the sounds together.

◆ If possible, visit a farm and see the animals firsthand.

◆ To the tune of "The Paw Paw Patch," sing the following song, and encourage your two year old to make the animal sound at the end of the fourth line:

> *The happy little cat lives on the farm,*
> *The happy little cat lives on the farm,*
> *The happy little cat lives on the farm,*
> *And this is what he says, "meow, meow."*
>
> *The happy little dog lives on the farm....*
> *The happy little horse lives on the farm....*
> *The happy little duck lives on the farm....*

◆ Continue with chicken, cow, pig, sheep and turkey.

 What your two year old will learn:
ABOUT ANIMAL SOUNDS

Little Froggie

◆ Two year olds love this poem because they can dramatize it very easily.

> This little froggie broke his toe.
> *(point to your toe)*
> This little froggie said, "oh, oh, oh."
> *(say "oh, oh, oh" very dramatically)*
> This little froggie cried and was sad.
> *(cry sadly)*
> This little froggie was thoughtful and good,
> *(fold your hands under your chin)*
> And ran to his mommy as fast as he could.
> *(your child runs to you and gives you a big hug)*

 What your two year old will learn:
CREATIVITY

Creatures

◆ Show your two year old pictures of a fish, a bird and a caterpillar.

◆ Talk about how each of these animals moves about. A fish swims, a bird flies and a caterpillar crawls.

◆ Pretend you are swimming like a fish.

◆ Pretend you are flying like a bird.

◆ Pretend you are crawling like a caterpillar.

◆ Recite the following rhyme and perform the actions:

> *Swim, little fish, in water clear,*
> *Fly, little bird, up in the air,*
> *Creep, little caterpillar, creep, creep,*
> *Sleep, little children, sleep, sleep.*
>   *(close your eyes and pretend to be sleeping)*

What your two year old will learn:
HOW ANIMALS MOVE

I Had a Little Turtle

◆ This familiar poem is a particular favorite with two year olds.

◆ Show your child pictures of turtles or, better yet, find a real one to observe.

◆ Place a toy turtle inside a large box. Recite the following poem and move the turtle accordingly:

There was a little turtle that lived in a box,
He swam in the water,
And he climbed on the rocks.
He snapped at a mosquito,
He snapped at a flea,
He snapped at a minnow,
And he snapped at me.

He caught the mosquito,
He caught the flea,
He caught the minnow,
But he didn't catch me!

What your two year old will learn:
LANGUAGE SKILLS

Two Little Blackbirds

◆ Say the poem and do the actions.

> Two little blackbirds sitting on the hill,
>   (hold up the pointer finger of each hand)
> One named Jack and one named Jill.
>   (wiggle "Jack" and then wiggle "Jill")
> Fly away, Jack. (wiggle your finger behind your back
>   in a flying motion)
> Fly away, Jill. (wiggle your other finger behind your
>   back in a flying motion)
> Come back, Jack. (bring Jack back)
> Come back, Jill. (bring Jill back)

◆ When your two year old can play the game and understands how to move his fingers, here is another variation.

◆ Pretend that you and your child are Jack and Jill.

◆ Recite the poem and act out the words.

◆ For the lines that say "fly away," find something in your house to hide behind.

◆ On the words "come back," come out from your hiding place.

 What your two year old will learn:
LANGUAGE SKILLS

See the Little Ducklings

◆ Fingerplays give your two year old practice in using different capacities of his brain. Doing movement and language together draws on both sides of the brain at once.

◆ Recite this poem with your child and do the actions.

See the little ducklings,
   (make a duck bill with the heel of your palms together)
Swimming here and there.
   (move your palms back and forth)
Heads are in the water,
   (make a headfirst diving motion with your hands)
Tails are in the air.
   (put your hands behind your back and wiggle them like a tail)

◆ You can also act out this poem.

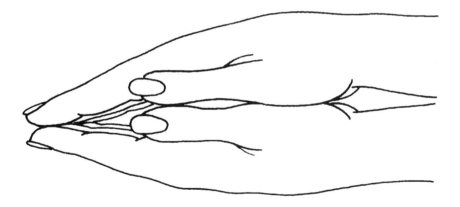

 What your two year old will learn:
COORDINATION

The Sticker Trail

◆ Little children love stickers and will want to play this game over and over.

◆ Find a place in your house where you can make a sticker trail on the floor.

◆ Make a path on the floor that ends behind a chair or sofa.

◆ Show your child how to follow the path to the very end.

◆ At the end of the path, have a doll or stuffed animal waiting for a hug.

◆ Pretend to be a dog woofing along the path. When you reach the end of the path, give the doll a hug and say, "Woof, woof."

◆ Keep repeating the game with different animals. A cat, a cow, a duck and a pig all make sounds that your two year old can make.

What your two year old will learn:
ABOUT ANIMAL SOUNDS

Happy, Sad Animals

◆ Your two year old loves to tell you what the doggie says and what the cow says, etc.

◆ Ask your two year old, "What could make a dog very happy?" The answers could be a variety of things: a new bone, lots of hugs, playing a game, etc.

◆ Pretend to bark with a happy sound.

◆ Ask your child, "What could make a dog sad?" The answers could be: no one to play with, not able to find a bone, etc.

◆ Try barking sadly.

◆ Continue this game with other animal sounds familiar to your two year old.

 What your two year old will learn:
ABOUT HAPPY AND SAD

Ten Little Chicks

◆ Two year olds are fascinated with farm animals and respond to any game that uses animals as a theme.

◆ Recite this poem and do the actions.

Ten little chicks on the chicken pen floor,
  (bend over and touch the floor with your hands)
Scratching for worms or something more.
  (move your fingers around on the floor)
Ten little chicks on a roost up high,
  (stand on your tiptoes and reach up high with your hands)
One little chick lets out a big sigh. (sigh)
The big brown eyes of the cunning fox,
  (bend side to side at the waist)
Sees the ten little chicks up on the box. (look up)
Quickly he jumps, but the chicks fly away,
  (jump up and run around the room)
And hide in their snug little nests all day.
  (curl up on the floor and pretend to be sleeping)

What your two year old will learn:
COORDINATION

The Stalking Cat

◆ This wonderful poem will help your child better observe animals and how they move.

◆ Recite the following poem and do the actions:

> When all the house is quiet,
>   (pretend to be sleeping)
> And the moon begins to shine,
>   (raise your arms over your head to make a circle)
> Out stalks the cat,
>   (get on your hands and knees)
> And this is what he finds.
> He walks around on silent paws,
>   (walk like a cat)
> Looking for mice everywhere.
> He swishes his tail and arches his back,
>   (wiggle your bottom and arch your back)
> He scares a mouse and says, "I like that!"
>   (lunge forward like a cat)

What your two year old will learn:
OBSERVATION SKILLS

Furry Squirrel

◆ Observe squirrels with your two year old and talk about the squirrel's bushy tail. Show a variety of nuts to your child and tell him that nuts are a favorite food of squirrels.

◆ Recite the following poem and do the actions:

I'm a fur, fur, furry squirrel
With a bush, bush, bushy tail.
And I scamper here and there,
Scamper everywhere,
Looking for some nuts.
  (scamper around the room looking for nuts)

I've got nuts on my nose, (put a nut on your nose)
Nuts on my toes, (put a nut on your toe)
Nuts on my head, (put a nut on your head)
Nuts in my bed, (lie down and put a nut next
  to your face)
Nuts in my paws, (hold a nut in your hand)
Nuts in my jaws. (hold a nut up to your jaw)
Crack, crack, pop! (Make a popping sound)

 What your two year old will learn:
CREATIVITY

Five Little Ducks

◆ This poem is very popular with young children. They especially like to make the "quack quack" sound.

◆ Recite the poem and do the actions.

Five little ducks that I once knew, (hold up five fingers)
Big ones, little ones, skinny ones, too. (make big and little
circles with your hands)
But the one little duck with the feather on his back,
(hold up one finger)
All he could do was "Quack, quack, quack." (move your thumb
up and down for a quacking motion)

Down to the river they would go,
Waddling, waddling, to and fro. (waddle like a duck)
But the one little duck with the feather on his back,
(hold up one finger)
All he could do was "Quack, quack, quack."

Up from the river they would come,
With a ho, ho, ho, and a hum, hum, hum. (waddle like a duck)
But the one little duck with the feather in his back,
(hold up one finger)
All he could do was "Quack, quack, quack."

What your two year old will learn:
LANGUAGE SKILLS

Elephants

◆ Look at books with pictures of elephants. The pictures in the Babar books are fun and will help your child recognize elephants.

◆ Show your child how to make elephant ears. Bend your elbow out and in, away from your body. Say the words "out" and "in" as you move your elbows.

◆ Walk around the room together like elephants and say the following poem:

> *I am an elephant,*
> *Glomp, glomp, glomp, glomp.*
> *I want some water,*
> *Glomp, glomp, glomp, glomp.*
> *Give me a peanut,*
> *Glomp, glomp, glomp, glomp.*
> *I am an elephant,*
> *Glomp, glomp, glomp.*

What your two year old will learn:
UNDERSTANDING OUT AND IN

Car Games

Zoom Zoom

◆ As you ride in the car, tell your child that every time you say the word "car," she can say, "zoom, zoom."

◆ Name things as you pass them in the car. "There is a man. There is a bus. There is a car. Zoom, zoom."

◆ Name three things at a time, with the third always being the car. "There is a house. There is a dog. There is a CAR! Zoom, zoom."

◆ Accent the word "car" and hesitate before saying it. "There is a...car."

◆ Soon your two year old will begin to anticipate the "car" word.

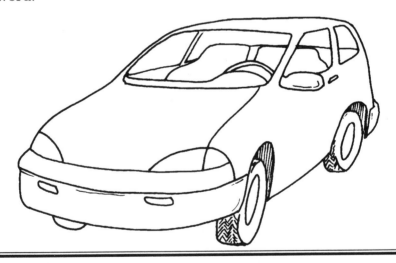

◆ What your two year old will learn:
LISTENING SKILLS

Sing the Word

◆ This is a great game to develop your child's listening skills and keep him occupied in the car.

◆ Sing the first line of a favorite song like "Mary Had a Little Lamb."

◆ Ask your child to sing it with you.

◆ Sing it again very softly until you come to the word "lamb." Sing that word in a louder voice.

◆ Sing it again, leaving out the word "lamb," and encourage your two year old to fill in the correct word.

◆ When your child understands how the game is played, try the second line.

◆ Soon you can sing the entire song with words left out for your two year old to fill in.

 What your two year old will learn:
LISTENING SKILLS

Oh, Hush-a-Bye My Darling

◆ Language games are fun to play in the car. Try reciting this poem to your two year old.

> *Riding in the car, car,*
> *Riding in the car, car,*
> *Riding in the car, car,*
> *Oh, hush-a-bye, my darling.*

◆ Say each line, stopping before the last word. Your two year old will soon learn to say the last words in each line .

◆ This time change the word "darling" to another affectionate term such as "sweetie" or "honey."

> *Riding in the car, car,*
> *Riding in the car, car,*
> *Riding in the car, car,*
> *Oh, hush-a-bye, my honey.*

◆ Think of all the different words that you can substitute for the last word.

◆ I was experimenting with this poem, and one child said, "Oh, piece of pie, my darling." She thought it was pretty funny, so we changed the last line.

 What your two year old will learn:
LANGUAGE SKILLS

Five Little Fingers

◆ As you are driving in the car, ask your two year old to hold up his hand. Tell him he has five fingers.

◆ Hold up your hand and wiggle each finger as you count up to five.

◆ Recite the following poem:

> *What can I do with five little fingers?*
> *What can I do with five little fingers?*
> *What can I do with five little fingers?*
> *What can I do today?*

◆ As you recite the poem, wiggle your fingers in the air.

> *I can shake my five little fingers,*
> *I can shake my five little fingers,*
> *I can shake my five little fingers,*
> *I can shake them today.*

◆ Here are other things to do with five little fingers.

> *I can wiggle my five little fingers....*
> *I can wave my five little fingers....*
> *I can pat with five little fingers....*
> *I can turn the wheel with five little fingers....*
> *I can beep the horn with five little fingers....*

What your two year old will learn:
COORDINATION

I'm Riding in the Car

◆ When you are riding in the car, sing the following words to the tune of "The Farmer in the Dell."

> *I'm riding in the car,*
> *I'm riding in the car,*
> *Heigh ho, the derry o,*
> *I'm riding in the car.*

◆ Point out to your two year old the various things you are passing by and what people are doing. For example: "People are walking."

◆ Sing about it.

> *I see the people walking,*
> *I see the people walking,*
> *Heigh ho, the derry o,*
> *I see the people walking.*

◆ Here are other things that you can sing about.

> *I hear the horns honking....*
> *I see a yellow car....*
> *I see a pretty house....*
> *I smell something cooking....*

 What your two year old will learn:
OBSERVATION SKILLS

Singathon

◆ Singing is a wonderful activity in the car. I can remember summer vacations where we sang the entire trip.

◆ Talk about songs that your child knows. You may be surprised to learn that she knows more than you realize.

◆ Practice two or three of the songs together. Tell her that when you get into the car, you are going to sing those songs.

◆ Once inside the car, remind your two year old of the songs you are going to sing.

◆ Say "One, two, ready, sing!" Have a great time!

◆ I've known children who refused to sing a particular song unless they were in the car.

 What your two year old will learn:
MEMORY SKILLS

The Whisper Game

◆ Riding in the car is a wonderful time to play the whisper game. Your two year old will be fascinated with his ability to change his voice.

◆ Say to your child in a normal voice, "I love you." Then say the same words in a whisper.

◆ Ask your child if he can say, "I love you" in a whisper.

◆ This may take a little practice, but soon he will understand.

◆ Ask questions in a whisper: "What does the cow say?" "What does the duck say?"

◆ Encourage him to whisper the answer. If he answers in a normal voice, whisper the answer yourself.

◆ Try singing a favorite song in a whisper. "Twinkle, Twinkle, Little Star" or "The ABC Song."

 What your two year old will learn:
LISTENING SKILLS

Peek-a-Boo Car

◆ Two year olds love to play peek-a-boo. This version is a little more sophisticated than the game you played when your child was a toddler.

◆ Playing this game in the car will keep your child busy and learning at the same time.

◆ Pick out something that you see from the car window: a tree, a car, people walking, etc.

◆ Ask your child to cover her eyes and play peek-a-boo with the car.

◆ Keep adding new things that you observe to play peek-a-boo with.

◆ Ask your child if she sees something for peek-a-boo.

◆ You can also play peek-a-boo with parts of the car like the horn, the steering wheel, the radio and the windshield wipers.

◆ To make the game even more fun, before each peek-a-boo, say "One, two, ready...go!" This gives your child something to anticipate.

 What your two year old will learn:
OBSERVATION SKILLS

Car Book

◆ In old magazines, find pictures of cars in different places: cars on the street, on the highway, in a store, etc.

◆ Cut out the pictures and glue them onto heavy paper.

◆ Staple the pages together to make a book about cars for your two year old to look at in the car.

◆ Give your child his car book, and as he turns the pages, ask questions about the book.

Can you find a red car?
Can you find a car on the street?
Does the car have a horn?
Can you find a pretty car?

 What your two year old will learn:
LANGUAGE SKILLS

Stop and Go

◆ There are two ways to play this game. To play the first way, cut two paper circles for your child to hold in the car.

◆ One circle is red and the other is green.

◆ As you drive up to a red light, tell your child, "I am stopping the car because the light is red. Can you hold up your red light?"

◆ When the light turns green, say to your two year old, "I am starting the car because the light has turned green. Can you hold up the green circle?"

◆ To play this game another way, draw and cut out a stop sign. When you come to a stop, ask your child to hold up the stop sign.

 What your two year old will learn:
COLOR RECOGNITION

The Wheels on the Car

◆ "The Wheels on the Bus" is a popular children's song. Change the words to "The Wheels on the Car."

> *The wheels on the car go 'round and 'round,*
> *'Round and 'round, 'round and 'round,*
> *The wheels on the car go 'round and 'round,*
> *All around the town.*

◆ You can adapt all the verses of the original song and make up some of your own verses. Here are some ideas:

> *The daddy in the car pulls up to the curb....*
> *The radio in the car goes off and on....*

 What your two year old will learn:
ABOUT CARS

Shapeagories

◆ This is a version for two year olds of the game "Categories."

◆ Cut out a paper circle and show it to your child. Tell her that when you ride in the car today, you are going to look for round shapes.

◆ As you drive along, point out circular shapes: a round sign, patterns on houses and doors, tires on cars, the steering wheel inside the car.

◆ Each time you see a circle, sing to the tune of "Frere Jacques":

>*I see a circle, I see a circle.*
>*It is a sign. It is a sign.*
>*It's a round circle,*
>*It's a round circle,*
>*It is a sign. It is a sign.*

◆ This is a good car game, but you can play it anywhere.

◆ When you feel that your child is beginning to understand what a circle is, play the game with a new shape.

 What your two year old will learn:
ABOUT SHAPES

Talking in the Car

◆ The car is a great place to have a guided conversation with your child.

◆ Ask your child to bring his favorite stuffed animal with him in the car.

◆ Ask him to show his teddy specific things: "Can you show Teddy the trees?" "Can you show Teddy the cars?" "Can you show Teddy the houses?"

◆ Continue with this kind of questioning.

◆ When you feel that your child is understanding you, add a new dimension to the questioning. First say the name of the object, then ask your child to show that object to his Teddy. For example: "There are the children playing in the park. Can you tell Teddy about that?"

◆ If your child does not understand right away, demonstrate for him: "Look, Teddy, the children are playing in the park."

◆ The next time you drive in the car, suggest that your child bring Teddy to show him things along the way.

◆ You will soon hear your child telling Teddy about different things that you see.

 What your two year old will learn:
LANGUAGE SKILLS

Who's That Singing?

◆ Two year olds enjoy listening to tapes in the car. Make your own tape to play in the car.

◆ Choose one song that your child recognizes, for example, "Twinkle, Twinkle, Little Star."

◆ Invite members of your family to sing the song one at a time while you record them on a cassette tape. You can also have your child's friends, neighbors, etc., sing the song onto the tape.

◆ Play the tape in the car, and see whether you can recognize who is singing the song.

◆ Another fun game for the car is to ask different people to say positive things to your child on a tape, for example, "You're such a nice boy."

◆ Let your child listen to these affirmations as you ride in the car.

◆ What your two year old will learn:
LISTENING SKILLS

Red, Green, Yellow

◆ Riding in the car is the perfect time to learn about stop lights. It is important to know what the different colors mean, and it will help your two year old learn her colors.

◆ Every time you come to a red light, say the following chant:

> *Red light, red light,*
> *What do you say?*
> *I say, "Stop,*
> *Hip, Hip, Hooray."*

◆ When the light turns green, you can say the following:

> *Green light, green light,*
> *What do you say?*
> *I say, "Go,*
> *Hip, hip, hooray."*

◆ For a yellow light, this is what to say.

> *Yellow light, yellow light,*
> *What do you say?*
> *I say, "Wait,*
> *Hip, hip, hooray."*

 What your two year old will learn:
ABOUT TRAFFIC LIGHTS

Art Games

Delicious Clay

◆ Make clay from the following recipe. Mix together:

> *One cup of peanut butter*
> *Three tablespoons of honey*
> *One cup of nonfat dry milk*

◆ Explore with your two year old all the different things that he can do with his clay.

Roll it into a ball.
Squash the ball into your hands.
Roll it into long skinny strips using the heel of his hand.
Make a ball and poke holes in it with his fingers.
Flatten it out and poke eyes, nose and mouth.

◆ Eat the clay for lunch.

What your two year old will learn:
COORDINATION

Shape Collage

◆ Choose one shape that you would like your two year old to become familiar with: circles, squares, triangles, hearts, etc.

◆ Cut that shape out of many materials: paper, foil, fabric and any others that you can think of.

◆ You will need a large piece of construction paper for your base.

◆ Put a dab of glue on the back of one shape, and show your child how to glue it onto the construction paper.

◆ Give your two year old the same shape cut from another material. Put some glue on it and let him put it down on the paper.

◆ Continue to give him one shape at a time until they are all used up.

◆ Compliment your child on what a beautiful job he did.

◆ Hang the collage in a spot where many people can view it.

What your two year old will learn:
ABOUT SHAPES

Rubbing With Crayons

◆ Gather together some objects with interesting textures: leaves, wood, rocks and buttons, for example.

◆ Remove the paper wrappings from several crayons.

◆ Place a piece of paper over one of the objects, and rub a crayon over the paper.

◆ Your child will be delighted with the results. It's almost like magic.

◆ Go outside and experiment with rubbings over tree bark, cement and anything else that you think would be interesting.

 What your two year old will learn:
ABOUT TEXTURES

Cookie Cutter Prints

◆ Cookie cutters have wonderful shapes for art projects.

◆ You will need a large piece of paper and some tempera paint.

◆ Show your two year old how to dip the cookie cutter into the paint and then "stamp" the piece of paper.

◆ He will love doing this over and over again..

 What your two year old will learn:
COORDINATION

Finger Puppets

◆ Your fingers make wonderful puppets. All you have to do is draw on them.

◆ Using a felt tip marker, you can make faces of any kind.

◆ Draw two eyes, a nose and a mouth on each finger of one hand.

◆ Recite the poem "Five Little Monkeys" as you wiggle one finger at a time.

> *Five little monkeys jumping on the bed,*
> *One fell off and hurt his little head.*
> *Mama called the doctor, and the doctor said,*
> *"No more monkeys jumping on the bed!"*

◆ Draw on your child's fingers and let her say the poem with you.

◆ When you are through with this game, wash your hands.

What your two year old will learn:
COORDINATION

Nature's Treasures

◆ A walk in the outdoors is always full of fascinating things to see and to hear.

◆ Your two year old is so curious, she wants to examine every leaf, stick and stone. This is a perfect opportunity to bring home treasures that you can continue to look at for a long time.

◆ Gather together your child's favorite rocks (small ones), leaves and sticks (small ones).

◆ Place contact paper on a wall or table with the sticky side out. Let your child stick her treasures on the paper to create a beautiful picture about nature. She will admire and talk about her picture for a long time.

◆ Explain to your two year old that if she removes the objects from the paper a couple of times, they will lose their stickiness.

◆ What your two year old will learn:
COORDINATION

Cotton Ball Art

◆ Lay a large piece of colored construction paper on a table.

◆ You will also need a package of triple size cotton balls and paste or a glue stick.

◆ Put paste on a cotton ball and show your child how to stick the cotton onto the paper.

◆ You and your child can do this activity together. It will encourage language development and bonding.

◆ Two year olds get a lot of satisfaction from this game and are very proud of the finished product.

◆ Hang the cotton ball picture so that everyone can view it.

 What your two year old will learn:
LANGUAGE SKILLS

Rain Art

◆ On a day when rain is predicted, lay a large piece of butcher paper outdoors on the ground.

◆ Find a place near a window from where you can watch what happens.

◆ Put different colors of tempera paint in small splotches all over the paper.

◆ Wait for the rain, and watch what happens to the paint.

◆ Retrieve the paper before all the paint has washed away.

◆ You will have all kinds of interesting designs and shapes.

 What your two year old will learn:
IMAGINATION

Draw Me

◆ Drawing excites your two year old and encourages his creativity.

◆ Your level of ability is not important, but your enthusiasm is.

◆ Tell your child what you are going to draw, maybe him, maybe your pet or something else. When you are finished, talk about the drawing.

◆ Gently outline your child's facial features with your finger. As you go around each feature, name it.

◆ When you are finished, draw the same features on your paper and repeat the names.

◆ For example, say, "I am drawing your eyes," and ask your child to touch his eyes. Say, "I am drawing your mouth," and ask your child to touch his mouth.

◆ Another kind of drawing experience that develops cognitive thinking is to draw outlines with your finger on your child's back. Try simple shapes at first. Circles and lines are the easiest.

What your two year old will learn:
BODY AWARENESS

Number Art

◆ Sit with your child and look through magazines for numbers. It is best to start with numbers "1" (one) and "2" (two). Catalogs, magazines and calendars are good sources.

◆ Each time you see a "1" or a "2," point to it and say its name.

◆ Cut out lots of the numbers.

◆ Let your child help you glue them onto a piece of construction paper. Each time you glue on a number, name it.

◆ Hang the collage in a prominent place so that your child can look at it often.

 What your two year old will learn:
TO RECOGNIZE NUMBERS

Painting

◆ Your two year old is ready to experiment with tempera paint or watercolors.

◆ One nice beginning is to put watery paint on a piece of paper, and show your child how to blow it around with a straw. This activity will help him see how colors change when they mix.

◆ Toothpicks make wonderful paintbrushes. Dip a toothpick into tempera paint and draw a line with it on some paper. Paint your child's name with the toothpick. He will be thrilled.

◆ Leaves and feathers also make excellent paintbrushes.

◆ Painting will make your child feel very proud of himself.

What your two year old will learn:
HAND-EYE COORDINATION

Paint Blobs

◆ This is a simple art game that is easy for your two year old and will give her a feeling of accomplishment.

◆ Put dabs of tempera paint on a piece of white paper.

◆ The paper should be fairly sturdy, like bond quality copy paper.

◆ The more colors that you use, the more interesting the final product will be.

◆ Fold the paper.

◆ Let your child move the paint around with her fingers. Encourage her to move her fingers all over the paper.

◆ Open up the paper and look at the beautiful picture.

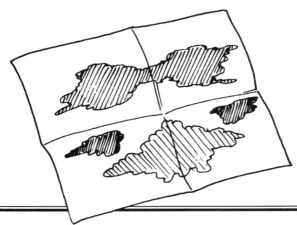

◆ What your two year old will learn:
CREATIVITY

Wooden Spoon Puppets

◆ Draw a face with a felt tip pen on one side of a wooden spoon.

◆ Cut a slit in the middle of a scrap of material.

◆ Put the spoon handle through the slit and tape the material to the spoon so that it won't jiggle around.

◆ Give your two year old the spoon puppet and show her how to move it around, move it up and down, and move it back and forth.

◆ Sing your favorite songs while moving the puppet around.

 What your two year old will learn:
CREATIVITY

Snowman Sock

◆ Stuff a plain white sock with facial tissue.

◆ Tie it in two places to create a head and a two-part body.

◆ Give your two year old scraps of material to help decorate the puppet. Talk about what would make a good mouth, two eyes, etc.

◆ When the puppet is finished, make up a simple story about a snowman. Try to use your child's name in the story.

◆ Sing snowman songs like "Frosty the Snowman."

◆ Hide the snowman. As you and your child look for it, sing this song to the tune of "Are You Sleeping?"

> *Little snowman, little snowman,*
> *Where are you? Where are you?*
> *I am going to find you,*
> *I am going to find you,*
> *Where are you? Where are you?*

What your two year old will learn:
CREATIVITY

Making Designs

◆ Think about all the ways that you can make a circle:

> *With your thumb and index finger*
> *With your arms*
> *With blocks*
> *By drawing around circular objects (a bowl, a cup)*
> *By drawing circles of different sizes with a crayon*
> *By placing your child in the middle of a circle of*
> *   stuffed animals*

◆ Each time you make a circle, say the word to your two year old.Look for circles in your house, in the yard or wherever you go.

◆ Take a large piece of paper for drawing. Give your child a crayon and guide her hand to make circles.Hold circular objects on the paper and guide her hand to draw around them.

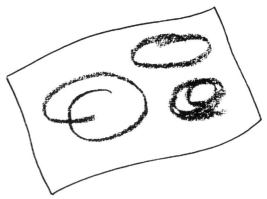

 What your two year old will learn:
IMAGINATION

Bunny Puppet

◆ Cut out a picture or draw a picture of a bunny's head.

◆ Tape the picture to the end of an ice cream stick.

◆ Poke a hole in the bottom of a paper cup and push the stick through the hole.

◆ The bunny's head should be sitting inside the cup. Your child can push the stick up and down and make the bunny pop out.

◆ Sing the song "Pop, Goes the Weasel," replacing the word "weasel" with "bunny." Let your child pop the bunny up on the words "Pop, goes the bunny."

◆ Here is a rhyme to say with the puppet.

> *Here's a bunny with ears so funny,*
>   *(point to bunny's ears)*
> *And here's his hole in the ground.*
>   *(point to the cup)*
> *A sound he hears,*
> *And perks up his ears,*
> *And pops right into the ground.*
>   *(make bunny go into the cup)*

 What your two year old will learn:
IMAGINATION

Counting Games

One, Two, Boo Hoo Hoo

◆ Young two year olds are beginning to get a sense of numbers. The more counting experiences they have, the sooner they will acquire the concepts.

◆ Hold up two fingers and say the following poem:

> *One, two,*
> *Boo hoo hoo.*

◆ As you say the words, point to each finger.

◆ Repeat the same poem, pointing to other parts of the body (of which there are two): ears, eyes, knees, elbows and feet.

◆ Once your child is able to play this game, look for other groups of twos in your house or yard, even patterns in clothes or on wallpaper.

◆ Give your child two blocks. Ask him to pick up the blocks, one at a time, saying the poem.

◆ Ask him to say the poem while putting the blocks down, one at a time.

 What your two year old will learn:
COUNTING

How Many Steps?

◆ Stand close to a door and say the following rhyme:

> *How many steps do I have to take*
> *To get from here to the door?*
> *Please count the steps I take*
> *Walking across the floor*
> *One....two.... (say the numbers as you take steps)*

◆ Repeat the poem while holding your child's hand as she walks with you.

◆ Repeat the poem, adding more steps.

◆ Experiment with the way that you step. You can take large steps, small steps, hopping steps, jumping steps, etc.

 What your two year old will learn:
COUNTING

Knee Bends

◆ Two year olds seem naturally to squat when they need to pick up something. Practice in squatting is excellent exercise for you and your child.

◆ Stand facing your child with your hands on your hips and your feet apart.

◆ Bend your knees and squat as you say the word "One."

◆ Straighten up again and say, "Two, see what I can do."

◆ Repeat several times, saying:

> *One, two,*
> *See what I can do.*

◆ When your child begins to copy you, add two more numbers.

> *Three, four,*
> *I can do some more.*
>
> *Five, six,*
> *These are funny tricks.*

 What your two year old will learn:
BALANCE

Counting Walk

◆ Take a walk through your house holding your two year old's hand.

◆ Start by counting chairs. Walk from room to room, saying out loud, "One chair, two chairs," etc.

◆ When you reach the number five, stop.

◆ On a large piece of paper, draw five chairs for your child to see. Count them again.

◆ Ask your child, "What would you like to count next?"

◆ Your child is likely to enjoy this game very much. It is best to keep the numbers fairly low, because two year olds lose interest if there are too many of any one thing.

 What your two year old will learn:
PRACTICE WITH NUMBERS

Bell Horses

◆ This is a lovely old English nursery rhyme to teach your child.

◆ Say the rhyme while holding your child's hand. Gently hold up one of her fingers on "one o'clock," hold up a second finger on "two o'clock" and so on.

> *Bell horses, bell horses,*
> *What's the time of day?*
> *One o'clock, two o'clock,*
> *Time to go away.*
>
> *Good horses, bad horses,*
> *What's the time of day?*
> *Three o'clock, four o'clock,*
> *Time to go away.*

◆ This game not only reinforces counting, but familiarizes your child with the names of numbers.

◆ Show your child how to make a "clip-clop" sound with her tongue.

 What your two year old will learn:
COUNTING

Me and You

◆ Recite the following poem with your two year old, touching the parts of the body as you name them:

> *I've got one head,*
> *One nose, too.*
> *One mouth, one chin,*
> *And so have you.*
>
> *I've got two eyes,*
> *Two ears, too.*
> *Two arms, two legs,*
> *And so have you.*
>
> *I've got two hands,*
> *Two thumbs, too.*
> *I'll wiggle my thumbs,*
> *And so can you.*

◆ This is fun to do standing in front of a mirror. Your child can see his head, nose, mouth, etc. as you touch them.

◆ Recite the poem again, holding your child's hand and helping him identify the parts of the body.

 What your two year old will learn:
BODY AWARENESS

There Were Three

◆ Recite the following poem. Each time you say the word "three," hold up three fingers.

> *There were three furry cats*
> *Purring by the fire.*
> *Meow, meow, meow,*
> *Purring by the fire.*
>
> *Count with me*
> *Three furry cats.*
> *Count with me,*
> *One, two, three.*
>
> *There were three yellow ducks*
> *Quacking by the road.*
> *Quack, quack, quack,*
> *Quacking by the road.*
>
> *Count with me*
> *Three yellow ducks.*
> *Count with me,*
> *One, two, three.*

◆ Other ideas include three big cows mooing in the yard, three little pigs playing in the mud, three little hens sitting on some eggs.

 What your two year old will learn:
COUNTING TO THREE

Four Little Puppies

◆ Talk about puppies with your two year old. Look at picture books and imitate the sound that puppies make.

◆ Recite the poem and do the actions.

Four little puppies scratched at the door, (hold up four fingers and move them up and down)
One, two, three, four. (touch each finger)
I gave them some food,
And they trotted out the door. (make your fingers walk away)

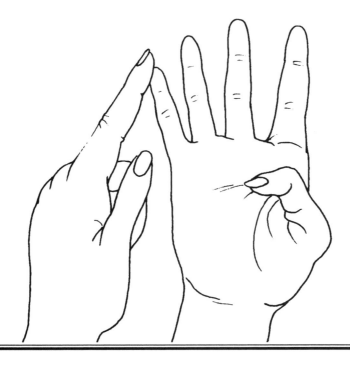

 What your two year old will learn:
IMITATION

One, Two, Crash

◆ When two year olds begin to play with blocks, they enjoy knocking them down as much as building them up. This can become a game that will develop fine motor skills and experiment with balance.

◆ Start stacking blocks and invite your child to continue. Talk about what you could stack next, but let your child make the decision. When you think the tower is ready to tumble (perhaps after only a few blocks), say, "One, two, ready, crash!"

◆ Encourage your child to knock down the tower, if she hasn't already done so.

◆ As you play this game, keep adding a number before "crash": "One, two, three, crash," "One, two, three, four, crash," etc.

◆ You can also count the blocks as you build.

 What your two year old will learn:
CAUSE AND EFFECT

One, Two, Three

◆ This traditional English rhyme is a lot of fun for two year olds. Say the rhyme and do the actions.

One, two, three, (hold up three fingers, one at a time)
Baby caught a flea. (pretend to catch a flea)
Put it in the teapot (pretend to put the flea into a teapot)
And made a cup of tea. (pretend to pour water from the teapot)
Oooops! (pretend the flea got away, and you are trying to catch it)

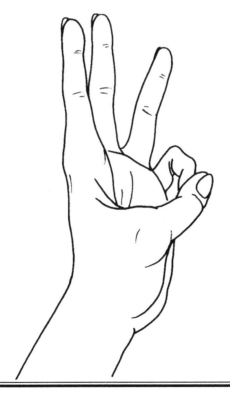

 What your two year old will learn:
CREATIVITY

Five Little Pigs

◆ This fingerplay will give your two year old practice in counting and a chance for self-expression as well.

One mommy duck taking a bath, (hold up one finger)
Taking a bath,
Taking a bath,
Just taking a bath. (pretend to be a quacking duck taking a bath)

Two little cats, (hold up two fingers)
Chasing their tails,
Chasing their tails,
Just chasing their tails. (run around the room)

Three little dogs, (hold up three fingers)
Rolling all around,
Rolling all around,
Just rolling all around. (roll your hands over one another)

Four little chicks, (hold up four fingers)
Pecking at the ground,
Pecking at the ground,
Just pecking at the ground. (peck at one palm with the other
*   pointer finger)*

Five little pigs, (hold up five fingers)
Rolling in the mud,
Rolling in the mud,
Just rolling in the mud. (make two fists and roll them over
*   each other)*

What your two year old will learn:
CREATIVITY

Three Little Pumpkins

◆ Hold up three fingers, and ask your child to copy you.

◆ Say the following poem.

> *Three little pumpkins*
> *Sitting on the wall.*
> *One little pumpkin*
> *Took a little fall.*

◆ Hold up two fingers and repeat the rhyme.

◆ Hold up one finger and repeat the rhyme.

◆ This is the last verse.

> *No little pumpkins, (make a zero with your thumb*
> *and forefinger)*
> *Don't you cry. (wipe your eyes)*
> *We'll take those pumpkins (hold up three fingers)*
> *And ,make a pumpkin pie! (rub your tummy)*

◆ Serve a pumpkin pie!

 What your two year old will learn:
COUNTING

Five Little Monkeys

◆ This popular children's rhyme will delight your two year old, especially the part where she gets to shake her finger.

◆ Recite the poem and do the actions.

Five little monkeys (hold up five fingers)
Jumping on the bed.
One jumped off and
Hurt his little head.
    (put your hand on your head and make a very sad face)
Papa called the doctor, (pretend to dial a telephone)
And the doctor said,
"No more monkeys jumping on the bed!" (shake your index
    finger as you say the doctor's words)

◆ Start the poem again with "four little monkeys."

◆ Continue on until there are no monkeys left.

What your two year old will learn:
CREATIVITY

There Were Five in the Bed

◆ Lie down on the floor on your back.

◆ Ask your two year old to lie down next to you on her back.

◆ Hold up five fingers and say,

> *There were five in the bed (hold up five fingers)*
> *And the little one said,*
> *"Roll over, roll over."*
> *So they all rolled over (both of you roll over)*
> *And one fell out.*
> *There were four in the bed (hold up four fingers)*
> *And the little one said,*
> *"Roll over, roll over."*
> *So they all rolled over (both of you roll over)*
> *And one fell out.*

◆ Continue until there are none in the bed.

> *There were none in the bed*
> *And the little one said,*
> *"Goodnight. Sleep Tight."*
> *(close your eyes and pretend to be sleeping)*

What your two year old will learn:
COUNTING BACKWARDS

Five Little Snowmen

◆ This counting rhyme is nice to do outside on a snowy day.

◆ Say the poem and do the actions.

Five little snowmen (hold up five fingers)
All made of snow. (pretend to roll a snowball)
Five little snowmen, (hold up five fingers)
Out came the sun (lift your arms above your head in a big circle)
And stayed all day. (keep your arms over your head)
One little snowman (hold up one finger)
Melted away. (make a wavy motion with your hands)

◆ Keep repeating the poem until there are no snowmen left.

What your two year old will learn:
COORDINATION

Wiggle Worms

◆ Hold up ten fingers for the worms. Each time two worms go away, place two fingers into your palm. Use the names of friends and family with whom your child is familiar.

> *Ten little wiggle worms sitting on a gate,*
> *Good-bye Mommy, Good-bye Daddy.*
> *Now there are eight. (put down two fingers)*
> *Eight little wiggle worms doing dancing tricks,*
> *Goodbye Billy, goodbye Johnny.*
> *Now there are six. (put down two fingers)*
> *Six little wiggle worms standing at the door,*
> *Goodbye Mary, goodbye Sarah.*
> *Now there are four. (put down two fingers)*
> *Four little wiggle worms mixing some stew,*
> *Goodbye Rex, Goodbye Tex.*
> *Now there are two. (put down two fingers)*
> *Two little wiggle worms standing in the sun,*
> *Goodbye Manny, goodbye Moe.*
> *Now there are none.*

What your two year old will learn:
FUN

Ones and Twos

◆ Saying the words "one" and "two," and being able to hold up one or two fingers, does not necessarily mean that a two year old understands the concepts.

◆ Experiencing numbers through all her senses will help your child acquire that understanding.

◆ Begin by talking about "a lot," "a few" and "one."

◆ Assemble blocks in groups of seven, three and one.

◆ Talk with your child about which group has a lot of blocks, a few blocks and one block.

◆ Ask your child to give you a block.

◆ Continue placing other objects in groups of a few, a lot and one. Stuffed animals and rocks are fun to use.

◆ Each time ask your child to give you one item.

◆ When you think that your child understands the "one" concept, begin introducing the concept of "two": two socks, two shoes, two hands, two eyes and so on.

◆ Play the same game, always including a group of "two."

What your two year old will learn:
UNDERSTANDING ONE AND TWO

Chalk Numbers

◆ Write out the numbers zero through ten in large print on the sidewalk.

◆ Use colored chalk, alternating the colors so that your two year old will see where one number ends and the next begins.

◆ Hold your child's hand and walk on the numbers. Say the name of each number as you step on it.

◆ Let her try this by herself. You say the numbers, and she does the walking.

◆ If she walks slowly, say the numbers slowly.

◆ If she walks fast, say the numbers fast.

◆ You can also write the letters of the alphabet or the names of everyone in the family.

 What your two year old will learn:
NUMBER NAMES

Oliver Twist

◆ This playground rhyme from Australia is excellent for familiarizing your child with the names of the numbers.

◆ The actions are fun, and he will respond to them.

◆ Do the actions as you say the rhyme.

> *Oliver Twist, can you do this?*
> *Oliver Twist, can you do this?*
> *Number one, touch your tongue.*
> *Number two, touch your shoe.*
> *Number three, touch your knee.*
> *Number four, touch the floor.*
> *Number five, jump up high.*
> *Number six, pick up sticks.*
> *Number seven, fly to heaven.*
> *Number eight, shut the gate.*
> *Number nine, hold up a sign.*
> *Number ten, begin again.*

What your two year old will learn:
LISTENING SKILLS

Teddy Bear Games

Pointing With Teddy

◆ Recite the following poem with your child and do the actions:

> *Point to your eye, (point to your own eye)*
> *Point to your nose, (point to your own nose)*
> *Point to your tummy, (point to your own tummy)*
> *And point to your toes. (point to your own toes)*
> *Hello, eye! (blink eyes)*
> *Hello, nose! (wiggle nose)*
> *Hello, tummy! (rub tummy)*
> *Hello, toes! (wiggle toes)*

◆ Take the teddy bear, and as you say the poem, let the teddy point to those parts of your child's body.

◆ Encourage your child to help the teddy bear.

 What your two year old will learn:
BODY AWARENESS

Hippety Hop

◆ Take your child's teddy bear or another stuffed animal and put it on a chair, sofa or the floor.

◆ Holding your child's hand, go to the opposite side of the room and say the following poem:

> *Hippety hop to the barbershop*
> *To buy a stick of candy.*
> *One for you and one for me,*
> *And one for sister Mandy.*

◆ You can change the words "sister Mandy" to "teddy bear."

◆ As you say the poem, hop to where the teddy bear is sitting. Pretend to give candy to yourself, to your child and to teddy.

◆ After you have pretended to give the candy, rub your tummy and say, "yum, yum, yum."

◆ Repeat the game, and each time you say the poem, move with a different motor activity: run, jump, march or slide to the teddy.

 What your two year old will learn:
COORDINATION

Dancing With Bears

◆ Show your child how to hold her teddy bear and dance around the room.

◆ Play different kinds of music for dancing.

◆ With slow music, glide or take very slow steps.

◆ With syncopated music, jump, hop or gallop.

◆ With fast music, run.

◆ When the music is finished, put the teddy bear down and say, "Thank you, Teddy, for dancing with me."

 What your two year old will learn:
RHYTHM

The Three Bears

◆ Tell your two year old the story of the three bears. Emphasize big, middle and small.

◆ The story should be a shortened version. Use different voices for each character.

◆ Each time you say, "Somebody's been eating my porridge," encourage your child to say the words with you.

◆ Get three teddy bears and tell the story again, using the bears as puppets saying each character's words.

◆ This is a wonderful language experience for young children.

 What your two year old will learn:
LANGUAGE SKILLS

Playful Teddy

◆ Line up several of your child's stuffed animals and dolls. Use teddy bears if you have them.

◆ Say this familiar poem using the words "teddy bear" instead of "elephant."

> *One teddy bear went out to play,*
>   *(walk into the middle of the room)*
> *On a spider's web one day.*
>   *(pretend to walk on a spider's web)*
> *He had such enormous fun,*
> *He asked another teddy bear to come.*
>   *(bring one stuffed animal to the center of the room)*

◆ Repeat the poem until all the animals are in the middle of the room.

◆ Hold your child's hand and walk around all the animals singing "Ring Around the Rosy."

What your two year old will learn:
COUNTING SKILLS

Itsy Bitsy Spider

◆ Two year olds adore the fingerplay "Itsy Bitsy Spider" and will say it over and over.

◆ Why not teach your teddy bear to say the poem?

◆ Ask your two year old to say the poem for teddy.

◆ After he has done this, have him take the teddy bear's arms and move them up and down as he says the poem.

Itsy bitsy spider went up the water spout,
(move your fingers upward in a crawling motion)
Down came the rain and washed the spider out.
(move your fingers downward like falling rain)
Out came the sun and dried up all the rain,
(make a big circle with your arms)
And the itsy bitsy spider went up the spout again.
(move your fingers upward in a crawling motion)

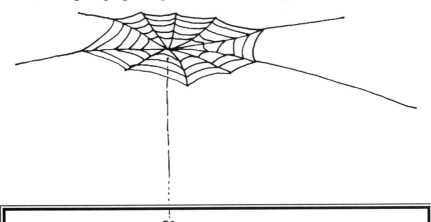

What your two year old will learn:
ABOUT UP AND DOWN

Grand Old Duke of Teddy

◆ "The Grand Old Duke of York" is fun for a two year old to play. It's even more fun when she can play the game with her teddy bear.

◆ Have your child hold teddy in her arms and do the actions to the following rhyme:

> *The grand old Duke of York,*
> *He had ten thousand men.*
> *He marched them up the hill and then,*
> *   (hold teddy in the air)*
> *He marched them down again. (bring teddy down)*
> *Now when you're up, you're up, (hold teddy up)*
> *And when you're down, you're down,*
> *   (bring teddy down)*
> *But when you're only halfway up,*
> *   (hold teddy in the middle)*
> *You're neither up (bring teddy up)*
> *Nor down. (bring teddy down)*

◆ Try saying the rhyme faster and faster, then slower and slower.

 What your two year old will learn:
ABOUT UP AND DOWN

'Round and 'Round the Garden

◆ This game is known as a "tickle game."

◆ First play the game with your two year old, then play the game with her teddy bear.

◆ Soon she will be playing the game with her teddy bear all by herself.

> *'Round and 'round the garden*
> *   (circle your index finger on her palm)*
> *Like a teddy bear. (keep circling)*
> *One step, two step,*
> *   (start walking your fingers up her arm)*
> *Tickle you under there. (tickle her under the arm)*

 What your two year old will learn:
FUN

Bear in the Cave

◆ Once your two year old has played this game, he will want to play it over and over.

◆ Have your child squat down and pretend to be in a cave. If you have a table with a cloth hanging over the sides, this makes a great prop.

◆ Say the words "bear in the cave" three times. Each time that you say it, make your voice a little louder. The fourth time say, "bear out of the cave" in a very loud voice.

◆ Your loud voice is the signal for your child to jump out from under the table and say, "grrr."

◆ You can make up other places to play this game: bear in the chair, bear behind the door, etc.

 What your two year old will learn:
LISTENING SKILLS

Teddy's Snoring

◆ Sing this song to the tune of "Are You Sleeping?"

> *Teddy's snoring,*
> *Teddy's snoring,*
> *Go to sleep,*
> *Go to sleep,*
> *Close your little eyes,*
> *Close your little eyes,*
> *Don't make a peep,*
> *Don't make a peep.*

◆ As you sing this song, your child and his teddy bear lie down on the floor and pretend to be asleep. You may have to do this, too!

◆ On the last two lines, sing the words very softly.

◆ After all is quiet for a few seconds, say in a loud voice, "Spring is here, wake up, wake up!"

◆ Your child and his teddy bear wake up and run around the room on all fours saying, "Grrrr."

◆ The surprise element of this game is very appealing to a two year old.

**What your two year old will learn:
LISTENING SKILLS**

Teddy Bears Are Creeping

A great getting ready for bed game

◆ Have your two year old crawl on the floor with her teddy bear. You can crawl toward the bedroom if it is bed time.

◆ As you crawl, say the following poem:

> *The teddy bears are creeping,*
> *Shh, shh, shh.*
> *The teddy bears are creeping,*
> *Shh, shh, shh.*
> *They never make a sound,*
> *As they go across the ground.*
> *The teddy bears are creeping,*
> *Shh, shh, shh.*

◆ This game also teaches children to speak in a soft voice.

◆ Make up other verses about the teddy bears, but always keep the middle two lines the same.

> *They never make a sound,*
> *As they go across the ground.*

◆ Some ideas for other verses are:

> *The teddy bears are sleeping....*
> *The teddy bears are crawling....*
> *The teddy bears are hopping....*

 What your two year old will learn:
IMAGINATION

Put the Bear

◆ Understanding the position of things develops your child's language. These relationship words help your two year old string words and ideas together.

◆ Place your child's teddy bear on a chair and say, "The bear is on the chair."

◆ Take the bear, put it under the chair and say, "The bear is under the chair."

◆ Ask your child to put the bear on the chair, then under the chair.

◆ Keep adding directions one at a time, still repeating the previous directions.

Put the bear in front of the car. (use a toy car)
Put the bear behind the car.
Put the bear's leg through the bed. (stick one leg through the crib)

 What your two year old will learn:
THINKING SKILLS

Movin' With Teddy

◆ Ask your two year old to hold his teddy bear and listen to the poem. Do what the poem says.

I hold my teddy bear and jump up and down.
I hold my teddy bear and hop off to town.
I hold my teddy bear and crawl to the door.
I hold my teddy bear and march on the floor.
I hold my teddy bear and what do you think?
We go to bed and fall fast asleep.
GOODNIGHT!

(show your child how to stare at his bear)
Bears, bears, bears,
Every, everywhere.

 What your two year old will learn:
TO LISTEN TO DIRECTIONS

Everywhere Bears

◆ Have your child hold his teddy bear and walk around the room with you as you say the following poem:

> *Bears, bears, bears,*
> *Every, everywhere.*
> *This little bear is climbing the stairs.*
>   *(child pretends teddy is climbing)*
> *This little bear is sitting on a chair.*
>   *(sit teddy down)*
> *This little bear is combing his hair.*
>   *(make the bear comb his hair)*
> *This little bear is eating a pear.*
>   *(pretend to be eating)*
> *This little bear knows how to stare.*
>   *(show your child how to stare at his bear)*
> *Bears, bears, bears,*
> *Every, everywhere.*

 What your two year old will learn:
LANGUAGE SKILLS

Mary Mack

◆ The popular children's chant "Miss Mary Mack" is fun to do with a teddy bear.

◆ Hold the teddy bear in your arms as if you were rocking it and recite the following poem:

> *Miss Mary Mack, Mack, Mack,*
> *All dressed in black, black, black,*
> *With silver buttons, buttons, buttons,*
> *Up and down her back, back, back.*

◆ Continue the chant with the teddy bear on top of your head.

> *She asked her mother, mother, mother,*
> *For fifteen cents, cents, cents,*
> *To see the elephants, elephants, elephants,*
> *Jump the fence, fence, fence.*

◆ Throw the teddy bear in the air as you say the next part.

> *They jumped so high, high, high,*
> *They reached the sky, sky, sky.*

◆ Rock the teddy bear again.

> *And they didn't come back, back, back,*
> *Till the 4th of July, 'ly, 'ly.*

 What your two year old will learn:
LANGUAGE SKILLS

What Do You See?

◆ Sit on a chair or sofa with your two year old and her teddy bear. Say "Teddy bear, teddy bear, what do you see?"

◆ Place the teddy bear on your nose.

◆ Say "I see your nose, looking at me." Tell your child to take the teddy and put him on the table.

> *Teddy bear, teddy bear,*
> *What do you see?*
> *I see the table looking at me.*

◆ Soon your child will get the idea and begin to put the teddy bear in different places in the room or on his body.

◆ What your two year old will learn:
LANGUAGE SKILLS

Teddy Quiz

◆ Hold your child's teddy bear and ask it a question: "Are you a happy teddy?"

◆ Move Teddy's head up and down in a "yes" movement.

◆ Ask another question: "Is the sun shining outside?"

◆ Move Teddy's head either "yes" or "no" depending on the weather.

◆ Give the teddy bear to your child and let her move the teddy's head to answer the questions.

◆ You can ask questions that really develop thinking skills. Here are some ideas.

> *Do dogs say meow?*
> *Did you have an apple for breakfast?*
> *Do you like to ride in the car?*
> *Can you turn on the light?*

◆ All these questions will cause your child to think carefully.

◆ What your two year old will learn:
THINKING SKILLS

Bears Come Marching in

◆ Tell your child to hold his teddy bear and make it march, jump, hop, run, etc.

◆ Sing this song to the tune of "Oh, When The Saints Go Marching In." Each time you sing the song, change the action word from "march" to a different motor activity.

> *Oh, when the bears,*
> *Come marching in,*
> *Oh, when the bears come marching in.*
> *I'm going to clap and shout "Hooray!"*
> *When the bears come marching in.*

◆ Your child can do the actions holding his teddy, or try to make the teddy do the actions.

 What your two year old will learn:
COORDINATION

Teddy's Birthday

◆ Having a birthday party for teddy is good to do a week or two before your child's birthday. It gives you a chance to act out events that might happen at the real party.

◆ Two year olds love having parties for anybody, and their help in preparing teddy's party will make their own party more meaningful.

◆ Bring teddy and all his stuffed friends into one area or sit them in chairs at a table.

◆ Think about what you will be doing for your child's birthday and try to do the same things for teddy.

A birthday sign—"Happy Birthday, Teddy"
Balloons around the room
Crepe paper streamers and other festive decorations
Gift-wrapped presents for teddy, maybe a lollipop, a book or a
*   toy that your child can play with, too*

◆ You could even have a birthday cake.

◆ And don't forget to sing "Happy Birthday!"

What your two year old will learn:
ANTICIPATION

Imagination Games

Building a Train

◆ Collect two groups of blocks, one for you and one for
your child.

◆ Invite your child to make a train with you. Put one of
your blocks down and ask him to put one of his down.
(Encourage him to choose a matching block from his
group.)

◆ Continue placing blocks next to one another.

◆ Talk about the train you are making together. Touch one
block and say, "This is the block that you put down."
Point to another block and say, "This is the block that I
put down."

◆ Play a train game with your child. Move the train of
blocks and say, "Here comes the train. Choo, choo, choo."

◆ When children have an opportunity to play both roles,
the leader and the follower, they begin to understand
what working together means.

 What your two year old will learn:
MATCHING SKILLS

Back and Forth

◆ Sit on the floor, legs apart, facing your child.

◆ Hold your child's hands and lean forward as your child leans backward.

◆ Now you lean backward as your child leans forward.

◆ As you move back and forth, say the words "back" and "forth."

◆ Once you have the rhythm going, sing a familiar song like "Row, Row, Row Your Boat."

> *Row, row, row your boat*
> *Gently down the stream.*
> *Merrily, merrily, merrily, merrily,*
> *Life is but a dream.*

 What your two year old will learn:
COOPERATION

The Piano Game

◆ You do not have to know how to play a piano in order to explore one with your two year old.

◆ Look at the piano keys and talk about the colors. Play a black key, then play a white key. Name the color as you play it.

◆ Play the keys on the upper right to make tiny raindrop sounds.

◆ Play the keys on the lower left to make thunder sounds.

◆ Make up a story about the little raindrops that fell from the sky. Play the upper right keys and keep going down to the lower left keys.

◆ Make up a song at the piano. Pick any two keys. Play them in a variety of ways: repeating, alternating, softly, loudly, with a pedal, etc. Make up questions and answers. For example: Play the first note and say, "How are you today?" Play the second note and say, "I am fine today."

◆ Encourage your child to play music on the piano.

◆ If you do not have a piano, use two musical instruments, such as a bell and a drum.

What your two year old will learn:
ABOUT SOUNDS

Singing in the Shower

◆ On a rainy day, this game is a nice substitute for being outdoors.

◆ Talk about the rain with your two year old. Talk about how people use umbrellas to keep the water off their bodies.

◆ Recite the poem "Rain, Rain, Go Away."

> *Rain, rain, go away,*
> *Come again some other day,*
> *Little _____ (child's name) wants to play.*

◆ Get an umbrella and step into the shower together. Sing rain songs like "Rain, Rain, Go Away," "Singing in the Rain," "It's Raining, It's Pouring."

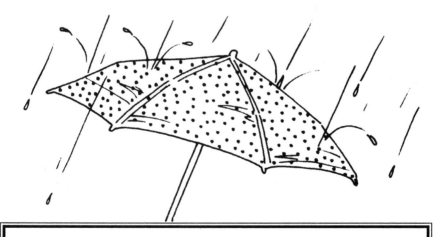

 What your two year old will learn:
FUN AND BONDING

Dressing Up

◆ Gather dress-up things for your child in a box.

◆ Scarves, neckties, hats, shoes and jewelry all work well, and your child will enjoy them very much.

◆ To get things started, put a scarf over your shoulder and a hat on your head. Change the tone or accent of your voice.

◆ Let your two year old try on whatever is in the box. He may put it on backwards or upside down. No matter, encourage and compliment him.

◆ Dressing up makes a child feel very special.

◆ When you compliment him about his choices, he will feel that his ideas are valuable.

What your two year old will learn:
HOW TO MAKE DECISIONS

Happy or Sad?

◆ Look through magazines with your child and talk about the expressions on people's faces.

◆ Point out happy faces and sad faces.

◆ Make a happy face and then a sad face. Ask your two year old to do the same.

◆ Tell your child some things that make you happy.

> *I am happy when I give you a hug.*
> *I am happy when we play together.*

◆ Tell your child some things that make you sad.

> *I am sad when a toy gets broken.*
> *I am sad when you are sad.*

◆ Recite the poem and let your child make the appropriate faces.

> *Once there was a little girl, little girl, little girl,*
> *Once there was a little girl*
> *And she was happy. (Child makes a happy face)*

◆ Repeat the poem using the word sad.

◆ You can add other words as well: silly, angry, mad.

 What your two year old will learn:
TO EXPRESS EMOTIONS

Sticker Fun

◆ Two year olds love stickers. Games that incorporate stickers keep their attention and give them lots of enjoyment.

◆ Take two tongue depressors and put a sticker on the end of each.

◆ Hold one sticker puppet in each hand. Put your hands behind your back.

◆ Bring one hand from behind your back, moving the stick up and down while you sing one of your child's favorite songs.

◆ Ask your child, "Would you like to see another puppet?" Bring out the other hand and move it up and down while you sing a different song.

◆ Give the stick puppets to your child and let him try to play the game.

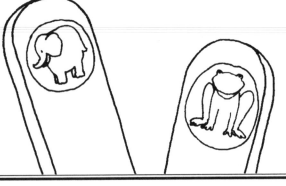

 What your two year old will learn:
CREATIVITY

A Glove Story

◆ Find a gardening glove or any glove that you do not mind drawing on. (This is a great game for using up those single gloves that have lost their partners.)

◆ Draw faces on the fingertips with a felt tip marker and give them names. They can be members of your family, animals or anything you choose.

◆ Put the glove on your hand and introduce the characters to your two year old.

◆ As you introduce each finger, tell who it is and say something in that person or animal's voice. For example: "This is Mr. Cow. Moo, moo."

◆ Ask your child to talk to Mr. Cow or to another character.

◆ If you are using animals on your glove puppet, sing the song "Old Macdonald Had a Farm."

◆ Another good song is "Five Little Monkeys."

 What your two year old will learn:
CREATIVITY

A Street of Blocks

◆ Two year olds love playing with blocks. They particularly enjoy putting them side by side.

◆ Encourage your child to make a long line of blocks. Tell her that you are making a street for the car to drive on.

◆ Get a toy car and push it along the block road.

◆ Your child will want to push the cars along the road as soon as she sees you doing it.

◆ Get more toy cars and trucks and push them along the road. Pretend to beep the horn and say things like "Look out, here I come!"

◆ Sing the following song to the tune of "Row, Row, Row Your Boat":

> *Drive, drive, drive your car,*
> *Gently down the road.*
> *Bumpity, bumpity, bumpity, bumpity,*
> *Look out here I come.*

◆ Add other blocks and stand them upright. These can be houses, buildings, the supermarket or whatever you imagine.

 What your two year old will learn:
CREATIVE THINKING

Spoon Talk

◆ Find a small plastic spoon that is easy for your child to hold.

◆ Draw a happy face on one side and a sad face on the other. Magic marker works well.

◆ Hold up the happy side and say, "I'm so happy, ha, ha, ha, ha, ha." Give the spoon to your child and ask him to repeat what you said.

◆ Hold up the sad face and say, "I'm so sad, boo hoo, boo hoo." Give the spoon to your child and ask him to repeat what you said.

◆ Talk about things you can say when you are happy or sad and the different facial expressions that show happiness or sadness.

 What your two year old will learn:
LANGUAGE SKILLS

Silly Peek-a-Boo

◆ Make a silly face. You could stick out your tongue, pull your lips apart with your fingers or scrunch up your face.

◆ Ask your child to make a silly face. Whatever he does, laugh and encourage him to do more.

◆ Put your hands over your face and say, "Silly, silly, peek-a-boo." Take your hands away and make a silly face.

◆ Ask your two year old to put her hands over her face. Say again, "Silly, silly, peek-a-boo." Your child will know what to do.

◆ After you have played this game a few times, make silly sounds to go with your silly face.

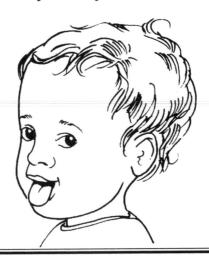

 What your two year old will learn:
IMAGINATION

Light On

◆ You will need a lamp with a foot switch in order to play this game.

◆ Say the words "Light on," turning on the light with your foot as you speak.

◆ When the light is on, sing a favorite song with your two year old. "Mary Had a Little Lamb" and "Twinkle, Twinkle, Little Star" are good choices.

◆ Now say the words "Light off," turning off the light with your foot.

◆ Put your fingers to your lips and say in a very soft voice, "Now it's time to be very quiet."

◆ Then say, "Light on" in a normal voice and play the game again.

◆ Soon your child will be saying the words for you. Two year olds really love to play this game.

 What your two year old will learn:
THINKING SKILLS

The Talking Room

◆ If you were a flower, what would you say?

◆ If you were a chair, what would you say?

◆ Thinking about something in a different way develops creative thinking.

◆ If your child is in your bed, you can say things like "Is this an elephant in my bed? Are you a lost little elephant?"

◆ Walk around the room with your two year old and talk to different objects.

◆ Ask questions of the objects and answer the questions in different voices.

> *Hello chair, what's the matter?*
> *Chair: I want someone to sit on me.*
>
> *Hello flower, you are very beautiful.*
> *Flower: Please, please, smell me.*

◆ This game is also excellent for developing language skills.

 What your two year old will learn:
CREATIVE THINKING

Animal Mix-Up

◆ Find pictures of several animals in magazines.

◆ Look at the pictures with your two year old and talk about how the animals look: are they furry, do they have four legs, are their noses big, etc.

◆ Cut out the animal pictures and mount them on construction paper.

◆ Cut each animal picture into two pieces and mix the pieces up. Help your child match the pieces.

◆ You can also mix up the pieces to invent new animals. For example: a cat head and a horse body could be called a cathorse.

◆ What kind of a sound do think a chickpig would make?

◆ What your two year old will learn:
THINKING SKILLS

A Sound Story

◆ Making animal sounds is something that two year olds do very well.

◆ Make up a story using two animals. Tell your child to make the sound that animal makes each time you say the animal's name in the story.

◆ Here is an example:

> *Once upon a time there were two little doggies (Child makes a dog sound). They lived in a house with two cats (Child makes a cat sound).*

◆ Continue on with the story, using each animal name three or four times.

◆ Once your child has learned this game, make up a new story with three animals or even four.

◆ This game will sharpen your child's listening skills.

 What your two year old will learn:
LISTENING SKILLS

Scarves for Sale

◆ Fill an empty tissue box with as many scarves as you can stuff into it.

◆ Say to your child, "Scarves for sale. Scarves for sale. Come and get your scarf."

◆ Let your child pull one scarf out of the box. Show him how to dance around the room with the scarf.

◆ Repeat "Scarves for sale," and let him pull out the next scarf. Have him dance around the room again.

◆ When all the scarves have been pulled out of the box, let your two year old put them back into the box. He will love doing this.

◆ As each scarf is pulled out of the box, tell your two year old what color it is.

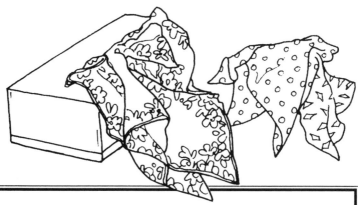

◆ What your two year old will learn:
FUN

Balloon Fun

◆ Blow up two balloons.

◆ Show your child how to bat the balloons in the air.

◆ After you have played with the balloons for awhile, tell your two year old that you know another game to play.

◆ Rub the balloon on your clothes to create static electricity and say:

> *Abracadabra ziggety zoo,*
> *Here is a magic balloon for you.*

◆ Stick the balloon on the wall or somewhere else that your child can reach.

◆ Repeat the chant, but this time let your child put the balloon on the wall.

◆ She will love this game and be fascinated with how the balloon stays on the wall.

What your two year old will learn:
LANGUAGE SKILLS

Acting Out a Story

◆ Older twos have favorite books that they love, and they have enough language skill to say words from the book.

◆ Choose one of your child's favorite books and dramatize it. Start with a story that is simple and repetitious.

◆ A good example is *Good Night, Moon* by Margaret Wise Brown. After you've read the book, say the words "good night" to everything in your child's room. "Good night, window. Good night, teddy," etc.

◆ Another favorite is *Caps for Sale* by Esphyr Slobodkina. Children love to imitate the monkeys.

◆ Shake your finger at your child and say, "You monkeys, you, give me back my caps." Encourage your child to mimic you.

 What your two year old will learn:
MEMORY SKILLS

Rig-a-Jig-Jig

◆ This popular children's rhyme is fun to do with your child. It creates a lot of possibilities for creativity and imagination.

◆ Hold your child's hand and walk around the room as you say the first part.

> *As I was walking down the street,*
> *Down the street, down the street,*
> *A little _____ (child's name) I chanced to meet,*
> *Hi ho, hi ho, hi ho.*

◆ Face your child and hold both of her hands. Walk in a circle as you say the next part.

> *A rig-a-jig-jig and away we go,*
> *Away we go, away we go,*
> *A rig-a-jig-jig and away we go,*
> *Hi ho, hi ho, hi ho.*

◆ After you have played this game a few times, change the person you chance to meet. You could meet a cow, a horse, a pig, an elephant, a cat, etc.

◆ Instead of saying, "a rig-a-jig-jig," say the sound of the animal. For example: "meow, meow, and away we go."

What your two year old will learn:
IMAGINATION

Nursery Rhyme Games

Little Boy Blue

◆ It helps young children develop good listening skills to practice acting out words they hear.

◆ Say the following nursery rhyme and act out the words:

Little Boy Blue, come blow your horn.
   (pretend to blow a horn like a trumpet, clarinet, etc.)
The sheep's in the meadow,
   (crawl around on all fours and say, "baa baa")
The cow's in the corn.
   (crawl around on all fours and say, "moo, moo")
Where's the little boy who looks after the sheep?
   (hold your child's hand and look everywhere
   for Little Boy Blue)
He's under the haystack
   fast asleep.
   (lay down on the floor and
   close your eyes
   as if you were sleeping)

 What your two year old will learn:
LISTENING SKILLS

Jack Be Nimble

◆ Say the following nursery rhyme to your two year old:

> *Jack be nimble,*
> *Jack be quick,*
> *Jack jump over*
> *The candlestick.*

◆ As you say the rhyme, hold your child's hand and, on the word "jump," jump with him.

◆ Try to stay very still until you say, "jump." This will not be easy.

◆ After your child understands the game, place a small object on the floor for her to jump over.

◆ Begin with a small block. Hold her hand and, on "jump," help her jump over the block.

◆ Add additional objects to jump over as she succeeds with each one.

◆ You can make an edible candlestick by putting a banana in a pineapple ring. Put a cherry on top to represent the fire. Repeat the poem and let your finger be "Jack" jumping over the candlestick.

What your two year old will learn:
COORDINATION

Jack and Jill

◆ Recite the nursery rhyme "Jack and Jill" with your child and act it out.

◆ Decide who will be Jack and who will be Jill.

Jack and Jill went up the hill
To fetch a pail of water. (hold your child's hand and
*   pretend to walk up a hill)*
Jack fell down ("Jack" should fall down)
And broke his crown, (put your hand to your head and
*   say, "boo hoo, boo hoo")*
And Jill came tumbling after. ("Jill" should fall down
*   and turn over on the floor)*

 What your two year old will learn:
CREATIVITY

The Three Little Kittens

◆ I remember loving this poem as a child. My children loved it, and I'm sure your children will feel the same.

◆ Say the poem and act it out in your own way. You will know what to do.

> *The three little kittens,*
> *They lost their mittens,*
> *And they began to cry,*
> *"Oh, mother dear, we sadly fear,*
> *Our mittens we have lost."*
> *"What! Lost your mittens,*
> *You naughty kittens,*
> *You shall have no pie."*
> *Meow, meow, meow.*
>
> *The three little kittens,*
> *They found their mittens,*
> *And they began to cry,*
> *"Oh, mother dear, see here, see here,*
> *Our mittens we have found."*
> *"Found your mittens, you good little kittens,*
> *Now you may have some pie."*
> *Meow, meow, meow.*

What your two year old will learn:
CREATIVITY

A Ram Sam Sam

◆ This chant from Morocco is fun to say and gives young children practice in making sounds.

◆ "Ram sam sam" is pronounced "Rum sum sum."

◆ Say the words and perform the actions:

> *A ram sam sam,*
> *A ram sam sam,*
> > *(make two fists and hit them together)*
> *Guli, guli, guli, guli, guli.*
> > *(put your hands together horizontally and pull them apart)*
> *(Repeat above)*
>
> *A rafi, a rafi,*
> > *(put your hands in the air)*
> *Guli, guli, guli, guli, guli.*
> > *(put your hands together horizontally and pull them apart)*
>
> *A ram sam sam.*
> *A ram sam sam.*
> > *(make two fists and hit them together)*
> *Guli, guli, guli, guli, guli.*
> > *(put your hands together horizontally and pull them apart)*

What your two year old will learn:
LANGUAGE SKILLS

Rub-a-Dub-Dub

◆ Nursery rhymes are short, with strong rhythm and non-sensical words. Your two year old will learn language through your repetition and enunciation. Be dramatic when you recite this rhyme.

◆ This is a good nursery rhyme for the bathtub.

> *Hey, rub-a-dub-dub,*
> *Three men in a tub,*
> *And who do you think they were?*
> *The butcher, the baker, the candlestick maker,*
> *And all had come from the fair.*

◆ As you name the three people, wash one of your child's hands for the butcher, wash the other hand for the baker, and wash her face for the candlestick maker.

 What your two year old will learn:
LANGUAGE SKILLS

Wee Willie Winkie

◆ "Wee Willie Winkie" is a charming nursery rhyme that children love to hear over and over.

◆ Recite the poem to your child.

> *Wee Willie Winkie,*
> *Runs through the town,*
> *Upstairs and downstairs*
> *In his nightgown.*
>
> *Rapping at the windows,*
> *Crying at the locks,*
> *"Are the children in their beds?*
> *For now it's eight o'clock."*

◆ Pretend to be Wee Willie Winkie. Run around the house and gently rap at the windows.

◆ Say the last two lines in a loud voice.

◆ Lie down and pretend to be sleeping.

◆ Practice this rhyme with your two year old and try to get him to say the last line. He will particularly enjoy lying down and pretending to sleep.

 What your two year old will learn:
LISTENING SKILLS

Roses Are Red

◆ Find pictures of roses and violets in magazines. Gardening magazines are very helpful.

◆ Cut out the pictures and glue them to heavy cardboard. It is good to have three pictures of roses and three pictures of violets.

◆ Show the pictures to your two year old and tell him the names of the flowers.

◆ Play a matching game. Try to sort the cards into roses and violets.

◆ Recite the familiar nursery rhyme.

> *Roses are red, (point to the roses)*
> *Violets are blue, (point to the violets)*
> *Sugar is sweet,*
> *And so are you. (give your child a big hug)*

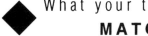 What your two year old will learn:
MATCHING SKILLS

Peter Piper

◆ Two year old children are too young to say tongue twisters, but they love to hear them.

◆ Listening to a tongue twister encourages them to make sounds.

◆ Peter Piper is a good nursery rhyme for making the "p" sound familiar.

◆ As you say the nursery rhyme, accent the "p" sound on each word. You will soon hear your two year old repeating the sound over and over.

Peter Piper picked a peck of pickled peppers.
A peck of pickled peppers, Peter Piper picked.
If Peter Piper picked a peck of pickled peppers,
Where's the peck of pickled peppers, Peter Piper picked?

 What your two year old will learn:
LANGUAGE SKILLS

Diddle Diddle Dumpling

◆ Recite this popular nursery rhyme to your two year old.

> *Diddle diddle dumpling,*
> *My son John (hop on one foot)*
> *Went to bed with his stockings on.*
> *One shoe off, (point to one foot)*
> *One shoe on, (point to the other foot)*
> *Diddle diddle dumpling,*
> *My son John. (hop on one foot)*

◆ Put one shoe on your child's foot.

◆ Repeat the poem and point to the foot with one shoe on and the one with one shoe off.

◆ Next time, put on both shoes. When you come to the words "one shoe off," take off one shoe.

 What your two year old will learn:
FUN

Hickory Dickory Dock

◆ Hold your two year old's hand and scurry your fingers up his arm as you say:

> *Hickory dickory dock,*
> *The mouse ran up the clock.*

◆ Gently pat your child on his head as you say:

> *The clock struck one,*

◆ Scurry your fingers down his arm as you say:

> *And down he run.*
> *Hickory dickory dock.*

◆ Switch parts and let your child play the game on your arm.

What your two year old will learn:
FUN AND BONDING

Ride a Cock Horse

◆ Recite the nursery rhyme and perform the actions.

Ride a cock horse
To Banbury Cross (pretend to be riding a horse)
To see a fair lady
Ride on a white horse. (stroke your horse as you ride
    around the room)
Rings on her fingers (wave fingers)
And bells on her toes, (shake feet)
And she shall have music
Wherever she goes. (pretend to sing)

 What your two year old will learn:
IMAGINATION

Hot Cross Buns

◆ Show your two year old a hot cross bun. Most bakeries sell them, particularly at Easter.

◆ Eat the hot cross bun and talk about how delicious it is.

◆ Teach the popular nursery rhyme to your child.

◆ Recite the rhyme and act it out.

> *Hot cross buns, hot cross buns, (rub your tummy to*
>   *show how delicious they are)*
> *One a penny, (hold up one finger)*
> *Two a penny, (hold up two fingers)*
> *Hot cross buns.*
> *If you have no daughters,*
> *Give them to your sons.*
> *Hot cross buns, hot cross buns. (rub your tummy again)*

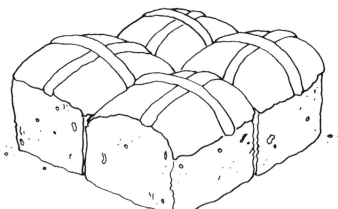

What your two year old will learn:
COORDINATION

Little Bo Peep

◆ The nursery rhyme "Little Bo Peep" is a lot of fun to act out.

◆ First, say the rhyme with your child a few times so that she will be familiar with it.

> *Little Bo Peep has lost her sheep*
> *And can't tell where to find them.*
> *Leave them alone, and they'll come home,*
> *Wagging their tails behind them.*

◆ Pretend to be a sheep and say, "baa, baa."

◆ Play a hiding game. Hide behind a door or chair and say, "baa baa." Your child will come to find you.

◆ Play another game with this rhyme. Put a shoe box on the floor and show your child how to jump over the box.

◆ Pretend that you are sheep coming home. Jump over the box as you "baa" and run around the room.

 What your two year old will learn:
CREATIVITY

Little Jack Horner

◆ Recite the nursery rhyme "Little Jack Horner" to your child.

> *Little Jack Horner*
> *Sat in the corner,*
> *Eating his Christmas pie.*
> *He stuck in his thumb*
> *And pulled out a plum,*
> *And said, "What a good boy am I."*

◆ Repeat the poem, pretending to stick in your thumb and pull something out. On the words "What a good boy am I," lick your thumb.

◆ Ask your child to join you in saying the rhyme.

◆ As your child becomes familiar with the rhyme, try acting out more of it. Instead of "Jack Horner," use your child's name. Sit in a corner and pretend to be eating a pie.

◆ To make this even sillier, instead of saying, "pulled out a plum," pull out other things:

> *Pulled out a banana....*
> *Pulled out a car....*
> *Pulled out a monkey....*

◆ Your two year old will have plenty of ideas.

 What your two year old will learn:
CREATIVITY

Little Miss Muffet

◆ The nursery rhyme "Little Miss Muffet" is fun to act out.

◆ One of you is "Miss Muffet" and the other is "the spider."

◆ Miss Muffet pretends that she is eating. When the spider comes next to her, she runs away.

◆ If your child is the spider, tell him to say, "boo," and then you run away. This is very funny to a two year old.

> *Little Miss Muffet sat on her tuffet,*
> *Eating her curds and whey.*
> *Along came a spider and sat down beside her,*
> *And frightened Miss Muffet away.*

◆ Another way to play this game is to change the last line of the rhyme.

> *Along came a spider and sat down beside her,*
> *And said, "What a very nice day!"*

◆ Think of different things that the spider can say: "Hello," "I love you" or "Let's go play."

 What your two year old will learn:
LANGUAGE SKILLS

Baa Baa Black Sheep

◆ Say the nursery rhyme "Baa, Baa, Black Sheep" to your child, emphasizing the last word in each line.

> *Baa, baa, black sheep, have you any WOOL?*
> *Yes sir, yes sir, three bags FULL.*
> *One for my master and one for my DAME,*
> *And one for the little boy who lives down the LANE.*

◆ After repeating the rhyme a few times, see whether your child can fill in the words at the end of each line.

◆ This is a good method of encouraging your child to speak. You can try this approach with any poem.

◆ Did you know that you can sing "Baa, Baa, Black Sheep" to the tune of "Twinkle, Twinkle, Little Star?"

 What your two year old will learn:
LANGUAGE SKILLS

Old Mother Hubbard

◆ Empty out a drawer or a shelf that your child can reach.

◆ Recite "Old Mother Hubbard" and act it out.

> *Old Mother Hubbard,*
> *She went to the cupboard*
> *To get her poor dog a bone.*
> *But when she got there,*
> *The cupboard was bare,*
> *And so her poor dog had none.*

◆ Add the following lines to the rhyme:

> *Boo, hoo, hoo,*
> *Her poor dog had none. (say this in a very sad voice)*

◆ Ask your child what he thinks the dog would like to eat. Whatever he says, incorporate it into the rhyme. If he says, "cookie," you can say, "to get her poor dog a cookie."

◆ Let your child act out the poem as you say the words. Always go to the drawer or shelf and open it to show that it is empty.

◆ Vary this rhyme by changing the name of Old Mother Hubbard to your child's name or your own name or by changing the dog to another animal.

 What your two year old will learn:
THINKING SKILLS

Humpty Dumpty

◆ Serve eggs for a meal. If you break the eggs, let your child watch as the shells crack.

◆ If you serve the eggs hard-boiled, let your child help you peel the eggs.

◆ Recite the nursery rhyme "Humpty Dumpty" and explain to your child that Humpty is an egg.

> *Humpty Dumpty sat on the wall,*
> *Humpty Dumpty had a great fall,*
> *All the king's horses and all the king's men*
> *Couldn't put Humpty together again.*

◆ Let your child pretend to be Humpty and fall down on the words "had a great fall."

◆ You can decorate a hard-boiled egg to be Humpty.

 What your two year old will learn:
ABOUT EGGS

Singing Games

Row, Row, Row Your Boat

◆ Sing the song "Row, Row, Row Your boat" with your child.

◆ Sing it again and pretend to be rowing a boat.

◆ Tell this story to your child.

> *Once upon a time a little girl named _____
> (child's name) was walking along the river.
> She saw a friend of hers and went over to say,
> "hello."*
>
> *The friend said "Hi, _____ (child's name), I'm
> going to go in a boat. Why don't you come
> along." They got into the rowboat, and what
> do you think they did??*

◆ Sing the song again.

◆ When you are sure that your child knows the song, try singing it with the last word of each line left out. For example:

> *Row, row, row your _____,
> Gently down the _____.*

◆ You will be amazed at how your child will fill in the word. This is a game that two year olds adore.

 What your two year old will learn:
LISTENING SKILLS

Greeting Song

◆ Sing this "Good Morning" song when you wake your child each morning.

◆ Sing to the tune of "Are You Sleeping?"

> *Are you sleeping, are you sleeping?*
> *Little _____ (child's name), little _____ (child's name).*
> *Now it's time to wake up,*
> *Now it's time to wake up,*
> *I love you, I love you.*

◆ You can change the first line of the song.

> *Where's your nose, where's your nose?*
> *or*
> *Are you hungry, are you hungry?*

 What your two year old will learn:
LISTENING SKILLS

Ring Around the Rosy

◆ Hold your child's hand as you walk with her in a circle.

◆ Sing the song "Ring Around the Rosy," and on the words "Ashes, ashes, we all fall down," fall to the ground while holding your child's hand.

> *Ring around the rosy,*
> *A pocketful of posies,*
> *Ashes, ashes,*
> *We all fall down.*

◆ While on the ground, sing the following words to the same melody:

> *Ring around the rosy,*
> *A pocketful of posies,*
> *Daisies, daisies,*
> *We all get up.*

◆ On the words "we all get up," stand up while holding your child's hands.

◆ Your two year old will want to play this game over and over.

What your two year old will learn:
FUN

This Is the Way

◆ Sing these verses to the tune of "Here We Go 'Round the Mulberry Bush." Do the actions as the words direct.

> *This is the way we clap our hands,*
> *Clap our hands, clap our hands.*
> *This is the way we clap our hands,*
> *So early in the morning.*

◆ You can substitute many other actions.

> *This is the way we jump up and down....*
> *This is the way we swing our arms....*
> *This is the way we stamp our feet....*
> *This is the way we click our tongues....*
> *This is the way we throw a kiss....*
> *This is the way we jump around....*

 What your two year old will learn:
COORDINATION

Sing Sing Sing

◆ Singing with your two year old is fun for both of you. Singing also will develop language skills which, in turn, develop pre-reading skills.

◆ Transition time is a good time to sing. Make up a song to "Here We Go 'Round the Mulberry Bush."

> *Now it's time to wash our hands,*
> *Take your toy and put it away.*

◆ Sing in the car, in the kitchen, while taking a bath, getting ready for bed—and don't forget a lullaby at the end of the day.

◆ The more a child sings, the better he will talk and read. Singing puts vowels and consonants in a rhythmic pattern just like words in a book.

◆ Whether it's "Twinkle, Twinkle, Little Star" or "Zip-A-Dee-Doo-Dah," enjoy singing with your child.

 What your two year old will learn:
LANGUAGE SKILLS

Put Your Finger in the Air

◆ The following words, sung to the tune of "Put Your Finger in the Air," offer a wonderful way to help your two year old learn the different parts of her body.

◆ Sit on the floor facing your child and talk about the different parts of the body. "Here is my nose (touch your nose) and here is your nose." (Touch your child's nose.)

◆ Repeat, touching yourself and then your child with your hair, cheek, ear, chin and toe.

◆ Say or sing these words and do the actions.

> *Put your finger on your head, on your head,*
> *Put your finger on your head, on your head,*
> *Put your finger on your head,*
> *Now is it green or red?*
> *Put your finger on your head, on your head.*

◆ Keep repeating.

> *Put your finger on your nose and see if it grows,*
> *Put your finger on your cheek and leave it there a week,*
> *Put your finger on your chin and let the food slip in,*
> *Put your finger on your toe and shake it yes and no.*

◆ Make up your own rhymes.

 What your two year old will learn:
BODY AWARENESS

You Are My Sunshine

◆ Hold your child in your arms and sing "You Are My Sunshine." What a wonderful message you are giving to your child about how much you care about her.

You are my sunshine,
My only sunshine,
You make me happy when skies are gray.
You'll never know, dear,
How much I love you,
Please don't take my sunshine away.

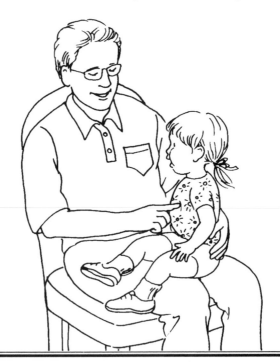

 What your two year old will learn:
BONDING

My Toes Are Starting to Wiggle

◆ Both you and your two year old take off your shoes.

◆ Show her how to wiggle her toes.

◆ Sing to the tune of "The Bear Goes Over the Mountain."

> *Oh, my toes are starting to wiggle,*
> *My toes are starting to wiggle,*
> *My toes are starting to wiggle,*
> *Wiggling all day long.*

◆ Pick additional parts of the body and sing about them as you wiggle them. Elbows, knees, fingers, nose and ears are fun to do.

◆ Try wiggling two parts of the body at once.

What your two year old will learn:
BODY AWARENESS

Clap Your Hands

◆ Show your two year old all the different ways that his body can move, like stamping, clapping, shaking hips, nodding head, shaking fingers and bending knees.

◆ Sing this folk song and do the actions with your child.

> *Clap, clap, clap your hands,*
> *Clap your hands together.*
> *Clap, clap, clap your hands,*
> *Clap your hands together.*

◆ Stamp, stamp, stamp your feet, etc.

◆ Shake, shake, shake your hips, etc.

◆ Bend, bend, bend your knees, etc.

 What your two year old will learn:
BODY AWARENESS

Swing Me Over

◆ This poem can be said while holding your child in your arms, swinging him back and forth, or while pushing him in a swing.

◆ Recite this poem in a sing-song voice or make up your own tune.

> *Swing me over the water,*
> *Swing me over the sea,*
> *Swing me over the garden wall,*
> *And swing me home for tea.*
>
> *Swing me over the treetops,*
> *Swing me over the zoo,*
> *Swing me over the garden wall,*
> *And swing me back to you!*

◆ On the words "swing me back to you," give your child a big hug.

What your two year old will learn:
FUN

Where, Oh Where

◆ Pretend you can't find your child and sing to the tune of "Paw Paw Patch":

> *Where, oh, where is my sweet _____ (child's name)?*
> *Where, oh, where is my sweet _____ (child's name)?*
> *Where, oh, where is my sweet _____ (child's name)?*
> *Come give me a hug.*

◆ Sing more verses and end each one with "come give me a hug."

> *Where, oh, where is your sweet toe?*
> *Where, oh, where is your sweet tummy?*
> *Where, oh, where is your sweet cheek?*

◆ With older two year olds who understand how to hide behind something, you can sing the song and look for them.

◆ You can also look for a toy.

◆ What your two year old will learn:
ANTICIPATION

I Don't Care

◆ By changing the words to the familiar song, "Jimmy Crack Corn," you can help your two year old become better coordinated.

> *Shake your arm and I don't care,*
> *Shake your arm and I don't care,*
> *Shake your arm and I don't care,*
> *Shake it every day.*

> *Shake your leg and I don't care,*
> *Shake your leg and I don't care,*
> *Shake your leg and I don't care,*
> *Shake it every day.*

◆ Here are more ideas to expand the song.

> *Wave your arm.*
> *Jump up and down.*
> *Bump your hips.*
> *Swing your arms.*
> *March, march, march.*

What your two year old will learn:
COORDINATION

Did You Ever See?

◆ This is a great activity for transitions as well as for listening.

◆ Make up verses to the tune of "Did You Ever See a Lassie?" Use your child's name in place of the word "lassie."

◆ This song has endless possibilities.

Did you ever see a _____ (child's name), _____ (child's name), _____ (child's name)?
Did you ever see a _____ (child's name),
Jump up and down? (Jump up and down)

Did you ever see a _____ (child's name), _____ (child's name), _____ (child's name)?
Did you ever see a _____ (child's name)
Give me a kiss? (Kiss your child)

◆ Here are other ideas.

Did you ever see a _____ (child's name) pick up his toys?
Did you ever see a _____ (child's name) bring me a book?
Did you ever see a _____ (child's name) touch his toes?

◆ This is a very open-ended game, and the sky's the limit.

 What your two year old will learn:
TO FOLLOW DIRECTIONS

The Muffin Man

◆ This is a favorite song for two year old children. They seem never to tire of it.

◆ This song will also develop your child's language skills and teach him a lot of information.

◆ Hold your child's hands while he is facing you, and walk in a circle as you sing.

> *Oh, do you know the Muffin Man,*
> *The Muffin Man, the Muffin Man?*
> *Oh, do you know the Muffin Man,*
> *Who lives in Drury Lane?*

◆ When you sing the next part, walk the opposite way.

> *Oh, yes, I know the Muffin Man,*
> *The Muffin Man, the Muffin Man.*
> *Oh, yes, I know the Muffin Man,*
> *Who lives in Drury Lane.*

◆ Repeat the song and substitute words. Instead of "Muffin Man," sing your child's name. Instead of "Drury Lane," sing the name of your street. You can sing about any person and where they live, about animals and where they live, etc.

 What your two year old will learn:
LANGUAGE SKILLS

Heigh Ho

◆ This familiar tune from "Snow White" has words that will remind your two year old about some of the things she does each day.

> *Heigh ho, heigh ho,*
> *It's off to work we go.*
> *We'll play with toys,*
> *And make some noise,*
> *Heigh ho, heigh ho, heigh ho.*
> *Heigh ho, heigh ho,*
> *It's off to work we go.*
> *We'll have a day of fun and play,*
> *Heigh ho, heigh ho.*
>
> *Heigh ho, heigh ho,*
> *It's off to bed we go.*
> *We'll brush our teeth,*
> *And wash our face,*
> *Heigh ho, heigh ho, heigh ho.*
> *Heigh ho, heigh ho,*
> *It's off to bed we go,*
> *We'll kiss good night,*
> *And close our eyes,*
> *Heigh ho, heigh ho.*

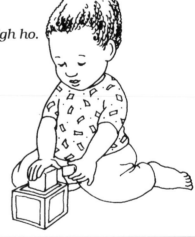

◆ What your two year old will learn:
SEQUENCING

Fleas

◆ The words of this song follow the scale up and down. Think of how you would sing do, re, mi, fa, sol, la, ti, do, and you can sing this song.

> *On my toe—DO*
> *There is a flea—RE*
> *Now he's climbing—MI*
> *On my knee—FA*
> *Past my tummy—SOL*
> *Past my nose—LA*
> *On my head where—TI*
> *My hair grows—DO*

◆ Now sing down the scale.

> *On my head there—DO*
> *Is a flea—TI*
> *Now he's climbing—LA*
> *Down on me—SOL*
> *Past my tummy—FA*
> *Past my knee—MI*
> *On my toe—RE*
> *Take that, you flea! (Say the words and tickle your*
> *   child's foot)*

◆ As you sing the song, move your hand up and down your child's body.

 What your two year old will learn:
TO SING THE SCALE

Let's Shake It

◆ Give your child two paper sacks and let him decorate them with magic marker.

◆ Fill the sacks with plastic blocks or metal measuring spoons and close them tightly with tape.

◆ Show your two year old how to shake the sacks to make sounds.

◆ Sing a favorite song while each of you accompanies the song with the shakers.

◆ Play different kinds of music and dance around using the shakers.

◆ Sing this song to the tune of "Mary Had a Little Lamb" and perform the actions.

> *Shaker, shaker, up, up, up, (shake above your head)*
> *Down, down, down, (shake with hands down)*
> *Up, up, up, (shake above your head)*
> *Shaker, shaker all around,*
> *All around the town. (shake arms in a large circle)*

What your two year old will learn:
RHYTHM

Jingle Bells

◆ The song "Jingle Bells" is one of the most popular children's songs of all time. Children love to sing and dance to it.

◆ To add to the enjoyment of singing the song, make shakers for your child.

◆ Get small bells at a crafts shop. Put two or three of these bells in a cardboard tube. Tape the container closed.

◆ Let your two year old decorate the shaker tube with crayons or stickers.

Sing the song and shake the bell shaker at the same time.
Sing the song slowly and shake slowly.
Sing the song fast and shake fast.
Shake the tube over your head.
Move your arm in a circle as you shake.
Shake the tube behind your back.
Sing the song soft and loud. The first part, which starts "Dashing through the snow," can be sung in a very soft voice. Sing the "jingle bells" part in a loud voice.

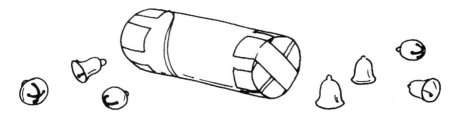

What your two year old will learn:
RHYTHM

I'm a Ghost

◆ Wrap white tissue paper over the end of your index finger.

◆ Put a rubber band around the tissue at your knuckle to make the head of a puppet. Draw a face on the puppet with a felt tip marker.

◆ Sing the following song to the tune of "The Farmer in the Dell":

> *Oh, I'm a flying ghost,*
> *Oh, I'm a flying ghost,*
> *Hi ho, the derry o,*
> *Oh, I'm a flying ghost. (wave your*
> *hand in the air and run around*
> *the room)*

◆ Ask you child to sing with you and pretend to be a ghost flying around the room. You can be a jumping ghost, a hopping ghost, a running ghost and more.

◆ Make a ghost puppet on your child's finger.

 What your two year old will learn:
IMAGINATION

Peanut Fun

◆ Shelling peanuts is a great activity to develop fine motor skills.

◆ Look at elephant pictures and talk about how elephants love to eat peanuts.

◆ Show your child some peanuts and explain how there is a surprise inside.

◆ Explain to your two year old that the shell is not good to put into your mouth.

◆ Give a peanut to your child and see if he can open it. If he needs help, suggest breaking it in half.

◆ Sing the song "Found a Peanut" to the tune of "My Darling, Clementine."

> *Found a peanut, found a peanut,*
> *Found a peanut just now,*
> *I just now found a peanut,*
> *Found a peanut just now.*

◆ CAUTION: Peanuts can be a choking hazard.

 What your two year old will learn:
HAND-EYE COORDINATION

In and Out the Village

◆ Whenever I play this game with two year olds, they want to do it over and over.

◆ The words of this song are sung to the tune of "Go In and Out the Window."

◆ Hold your child's hand. As you sing "go in and out the village," run forward and backward.

> *Go in and out the village,*
> *Go in and out the village,*
> *Go in and out the village,*
> *As you have done before. (clap your hands together)*

◆ On the next part, reach up high and bend down low.

> *Go up and down the village,*
> *Go up and down the village,*
> *Go up and down the village,*
> *As you have done before. (clap your hands together)*

◆ This time walk around in a circle.

> *Go 'round and 'round the village,*
> *Go 'round and 'round the village,*
> *Go 'round and 'round the village,*
> *As you have done before. (clap your hands together)*

What your two year old will learn:
COORDINATION

Cooking Games

The Edible Snowman

◆ Place two scoops of vanilla ice cream one on top of the other.

◆ Set out a variety of nuts, raisins and interesting cereal shapes on waxed paper.

◆ Encourage your child to make a face on the ice cream snowman. She may prefer to put the goodies all over the ice cream. Either way, you will stimulate her creative juices.

◆ Try a cookie with a marshmallow on top for a hat.

◆ Not only does this game encourage creativity, but it provides experiences of sensing, design and form. And it's yummy to eat!

 What your two year old will learn:
CREATIVITY

Pizza Fun

◆ Buy a ready-made pizza crust.

◆ Go to your local salad bar and pick out a variety of sliced vegetables and cheeses to decorate your pizza: green and red peppers, olives, shredded cheese, carrot strips, celery strips, pineapple chunks and raisins, for example.

◆ Show your child how to sprinkle cheese on top of the pizza crust.

◆ Put out all of the salad ingredients, and let your child decorate the pizza any way that she wants.If you desire, add sauce before the toppings.

◆ Put in the oven, bake and enjoy.

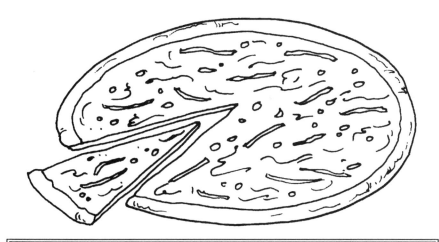

 What your two year old will learn:
CREATIVITY

Making Caterpillars

◆ Cut several grapes in half.

◆ Put the grape halves in a straight line on a plate to make a caterpillar.

◆ Place raisins on each side of the grapes to make feet.

◆ Put two raisins at one end to give the caterpillar eyes.

◆ Recite the following poem, "Arabella Miller."

> *Little Arabella Miller,*
> *Found a furry caterpillar.*
> *First it crawled upon her mother,*
> *Then upon her baby brother.*
> *Both cried, "Naughty Arabella,*
> *Put away that caterpillar."*

◆ Eat the grape caterpillar.

 What your two year old will learn:
CREATIVITY

Body Food

◆ Talk with your two year old about the parts of his face. Questions like "Where is your nose?" "Where are your eyes?" will bring delight to your child.

◆ Draw a large circle on a piece of paper and draw the parts of the face that you talked about with your child.

◆ Slice an orange so as to make a circle. Using raisins for eyes, nuts for the nose and a pimento for the mouth, show your two year old how to make a face on the orange slice. Eat this yummy face!

◆ Cut several more slices and let your child make faces by himself.

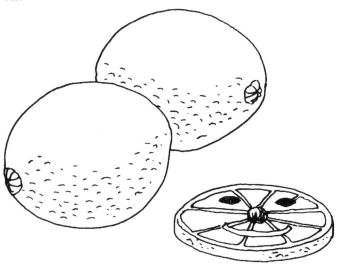

 What your two year old will learn:
BODY AWARENESS

Berry Nice

◆ A variety of berries are often available at the supermarket. Berries have such interesting flavors and textures and are nutritious as well.

◆ Select two kinds of berries of different color and texture, for example, blueberries and strawberries.

◆ Show your child how to wash the berries and pat them dry.

◆ Sort them into two piles, naming them as you sort.

◆ Let your child taste the berries.

◆ Pour vanilla yogurt into a dish.

◆ Ask your two year old to add the berries to the yogurt.

◆ Eat and enjoy.

 What your two year old will learn:
SELF-HELP SKILLS

Banana Treats

◆ Tell your child a story about a monkey whose name was _____ (child's name), who swung from tree to tree looking for bananas.

◆ Pretend to swing from a tree and make monkey sounds. Pretend to find a banana and peel it.

◆ Go into the kitchen and give your two year old a banana to peel. He may need a little help.

◆ Using a plastic knife, help your child slice the banana.

◆ You can roll the banana slices in cinnamon and nuts.

◆ You can mix the banana with cereal, raisins or yogurt.

◆ You can make a banana milk shake by mixing it with ice cream or yogurt in a blender.

 What your two year old will learn:
SELF-HELP SKILLS

Do It Yourself Cereal

◆ Your child is becoming more independent and wants to do things for himself.

◆ This is the "me do it" age, and whenever you can provide this opportunity, it will help him feel good about himself.

◆ If you measure out various ingredients for cereal, your two year old can pour them into a bowl and stir them up.

◆ Place three or four ingredients in small bowls, for example, dry cereal, raisins, nuts and wheat germ.

◆ Give your child a larger bowl and tell him to pour the smaller bowls into it.

◆ Sing this song to the tune of "Frere Jacques," as you pour each small bowl.

> *Take the raisins, take the raisins,*
> *Pour them in, pour them in.*
> *We are going to eat them,*
> *We are going to eat them,*
> *Yum, yum, yum.*
> *Yum, yum, yum.*

◆ When all the bowls are poured, add milk, stir and eat!

 What your two year old will learn:
SELF-HELP SKILLS

Sponges

◆ Cooking is fun to do with two year olds. Cleaning up the mess can be fun, too.

◆ Put out two bowls. Fill one with water and leave the other one empty.

◆ Show your child how to dip a sponge into the water-filled bowl and squeeze it out into the empty one.

◆ Your child will love doing this and will remain at this activity for a long time.

◆ When you see that she is getting at all bored, show her how to squeeze out the sponge and wipe things.

◆ Give her specific items to wipe: "Please wipe the table-top." "Please wipe the sink."

◆ By learning how to squeeze first, she will understand that in order to wipe something, she must squeeze out the water.

 What your two year old will learn:
SELF-HELP SKILLS

Sweet Potato Games

◆ Show your child a sweet potato. Let her feel it, smell it and roll it in her hands.

◆ Cook the sweet potato and let her taste it. Microwaving is the fastest way to cook the potato.

◆ Try growing a sweet potato plant. Stick three or four toothpicks into the sides of the sweet potato so that it will balance in a glass.

◆ Put the sweet potato in a glass and cover the bottom part with water. Check the potato each day to be sure there is enough water.

◆ When the sprouts appear, your two year old will be delighted.

◆ Recite this poem to your child.

> *Sweet potato, sweet potato, sweet potato pie,*
> *If I don't get some, I think I'm gonna die.*
> *Give me, give me some sweet potato pie,*
> *Come here you sweet potato! (hug your child)*

 What your two year old will learn:
TO TASTE NEW FOODS

Sorting Crackers

◆ Put an assortment of crackers on a place mat. Select interesting shapes and sizes.

◆ Prepare a place mat for your child and one for yourself.

◆ Pick up a cracker and talk about its shape, size and smell.

◆ Ask your child to find a matching cracker on his place mat. Praise him when he matches correctly.

◆ After you have matched all the crackers, mix them up and play again.

◆ Set out cream cheese, softened margarine or peanut butter. Let your child spread something on the cracker if he desires.

 What your two year old will learn:
MATCHING SKILLS

Roly-Poly Sandwiches

◆ Cut the crusts off two slices of whole wheat bread.

◆ Put peanut butter, jelly, honey and cinnamon on the table.

◆ Show your child how to use a rolling pin to flatten the bread.

◆ Ask your child to spread peanut butter on the bread and to choose whatever else he would like as well.

◆ While he is spreading his bread, spread yours to model the process.

◆ Help your child roll up the sandwich like a jelly roll.

◆ Cut the roll into three or four slices and insert a toothpick to hold them together.

◆ Your two year old will be fascinated with the design in the middle and will love eating the sandwich.

 What your two year old will learn:
COORDINATION

Oh Boy, Kebabs!

◆ Select several of your child's favorite fruits and vegetables and cut them into chunks.

◆ Use apples, bananas, pears, cucumbers, carrots, celery, strawberries and any other fruit or vegetable that is easily skewered.

◆ Show your child how to make a kebab by threading the chunks onto a wooden skewer or long toothpick.

◆ As he puts the pieces onto the skewer, name the fruit or vegetable and say something positive about it. For example: "That's an apple. It tastes sweet and crunchy."

◆ When your child hears you describe a fruit or vegetable in a positive way, he will develop a positive attitude about it.

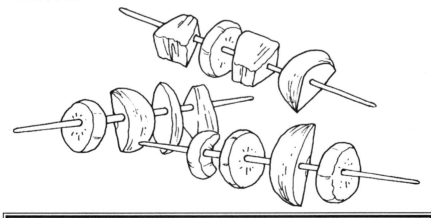

 What your two year old will learn:
COORDINATION

Alligator Avocado

◆ In Mexico, the avocado is called an "alligator pear."

◆ Show your child an avocado and explain how the seed is inside.

◆ Say the following poem and do the actions:

Alligator, alligator, you look so mean. (make a mean face)
Alligator, alligator, you are green. (point to something green)
You live in the water, (make a swimming motion)
And on the land. (walk in a circle)
I better be careful,
And watch where I stand! (look around for alligators)

◆ Make guacamole with your child. Mix together avocado, lemon juice, diced tomato, one tablespoon of mayonnaise, minced onion and garlic salt.

◆ Eat with raw vegetables or crackers.

What your two year old will learn:
COORDINATION

Eggs

◆ This simple fingerplay will help your two year old understand how eggs are cooked.

◆ Recite the poem and hold up the correct finger.

> Mommy bought an egg. *(little finger)*
> Daddy cracked it open. *(ring finger)*
> Sister put it in the pan. *(middle finger)*
> Brother cooked it. *(index finger)*
> And this little fellow ate it all up. *(thumb)*

◆ You can use the names of friends, relatives and even your animals.

◆ Talk about all the different ways that you can cook eggs. Choose one way—over easy, hard-boiled, poached or scrambled—and show your child how to cook the egg.

 What your two year old will learn:
LISTENING SKILLS

Pumpkin Fun

◆ Carving a pumpkin is always a lot of fun for everyone. Your two year old will delight in seeing the inside of a pumpkin as well as in the face that you carve.

◆ After scooping the inside of the pumpkin, save the seeds for another treat.

◆ With your child's help, wash the pumpkin seeds and put them on a cookie sheet to dry.

◆ Bake them in a 300 degree oven until they are brown. This will take about 20 minutes.

◆ Let your two year old shake salt on the seeds. Eat them and enjoy!

◆ While you are doing these pumpkin activities, you can say the popular nursery rhyme.

> *Peter, Peter, pumpkin eater,*
> *Had a wife and couldn't keep her.*
> *He put her in a pumpkin shell,*
> *And there he kept her very well.*

 What your two year old will learn:
ABOUT PUMPKINS

Rudolph Sandwich

◆ The song "Rudolph the Red-Nosed Reindeer" is very popular with two year olds.

◆ Everyone will enjoy making a Rudolph treat.

◆ Cut a piece of bread into two triangles.

◆ Let your child spread the triangles with butter, peanut butter or cream cheese.

◆ Stick pretzels into the bread for antlers.

◆ Put out a variety of items for eyes, nose and mouth: raisins, pepper slices, olives, tomatoes and nuts. Let your two year old decide which to use.

◆ When you are finished, sing the song "Rudolph the Red-Nosed Reindeer."

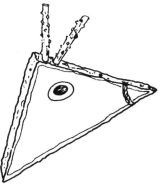

 What your two year old will learn:
CREATIVITY

The Bean Brigade

◆ According to the new food guidelines beans are a nutritious and excellent choice.

◆ There are so many kinds of beans, of many colors, shapes and sizes.

◆ Select several kinds and mix them together in a bowl.

◆ Help your two year old sort the beans into different groups. As you sort together, talk about the sizes, the colors and the shapes.

◆ When all the beans have been sorted, wash them. Your child will enjoy doing this very much.

◆ Put them into a pot and cover them with water.

◆ Add a variety of vegetables and canned tomatoes. Let it cook until the beans are tender.

◆ Voila! Bean soup.

◆ CAUTION: Closely supervise the sorting and handling of beans by your two year old, especially if he still puts things into his mouth.

 What your two year old will learn:
SORTING SKILLS

Red Food

◆ Your older two year old loves to learn about colors.

◆ Your child can help you prepare red foods while at the same time learning their names and how they taste.

◆ Tomato juice and cranberry juice are very tasty. Let your child pour the juice for a snack. Tomatoes are delicious, and your child can help wash them.

◆ Many fruits are red. Apples, strawberries, plums and cherries. Your child can help wash and arrange them on a plate. You might want to pit the cherries first.

◆ As you try each food, sing to the tune of "Are You Sleeping?"

I am eating, I am eating
Something red, something red.
It is so delicious,
It is so delicious,
Yum, yum, yum.
Yum, yum, yum.

 What your two year old will learn:
ABOUT THE COLOR RED

Making Butter

◆ Making butter with your two year old is fascinating for him and lots of fun for both of you.

◆ Look at pictures of cows, make "moo" sounds and talk about how the cow gives us milk.

◆ Fill a jar half full of whipping cream or heavy cream.

◆ Shake the jar vigorously. Let your child shake, too.

◆ When you see the cream begin to separate, pour off the liquid.

◆ Continue shaking until a ball of butter is formed, then rinse the butter a few times, or until you see that the liquid is almost clear.

◆ As you rinse the butter, whip it with a spoon.

◆ Add salt to the butter and spread it on your favorite crackers.

What your two year old will learn:
HOW BUTTER IS MADE

Nature Games

Making a Trail

◆ Go for a walk with your child. As you go along, tie crepe paper streamers on landmarks—a tree, a lamp post or a fence.

◆ Let your child help you tie the streamers so that she will better remember where they are.

◆ After you have gone about two blocks, tell your child, "Now we are going home, and the streamers will help us find our way."

◆ As you return, untie the streamers.

◆ A nice idea is to count the streamers as you tie them and as you return.

◆ If you walk along a beach, or play the game in the snow, you can use footprints to find your way back.

 What your two year old will learn:
OBSERVATION SKILLS

Inside Snow

◆ Why not bring snow inside, and let your two year old play with it.

◆ Here are things that you can do with snow:

> *Spoon it into a dish.*
> *Color it with food coloring.*
> *Watch it melt.*
> *Make little snowballs.*
> *Make a miniature snowman and put it in the freezer.*

◆ Sing the following song to the tune of "London Bridge Is Falling Down":

> *It is snowing in my house, in my house, in my house,*
> *It is snowing in my house,*
> *I like snow.*

 What your two year old will learn:
ABOUT SNOW

Everything Grows

◆ Do the following activity and ask your child to copy you.

◆ Cup your hands above your head, kneel and say:

"I am a little flower, and I'm growing and growing and growing."

◆ As you say these words, slowly lift your body upward, stretching taller.

◆ Hug your body with your arms, kneel and say:

"I'm an oak tree, and I am growing and growing and growing."

◆ As you say these words, slowly rise up, standing up on your toes as you stretch your arms out like branches.

◆ Kneel again and say:

"I'm a little _____ (child's name), and I am growing and growing and growing."

◆ As you say these words, jump up as high as you can.

 What your two year old will learn:
ABOUT GROWING

A Sound Walk

◆ Two year old children are inquisitive about everything that they see and hear. This game develops their awareness of the environment.

◆ Walk outside with your child and listen for sounds around you:

> *Wind blowing*
> *Birds chirping*
> *Leaves rustling*
> *Cars driving*
> *Dogs barking*
> *People talking*

◆ Talk about the sounds with your child, and see if you can imitate them.

◆ What your two year old will learn:
LISTENING SKILLS

Where Do You Think the Birdie Lives?

◆ When you are outdoors, observe the birds and talk about where they live, the sounds that they make and their color.

◆ Here is a fingerplay to do with your two year old that both of you will enjoy.

◆ Hold your child's palm facing you. As you say the rhyme, take your hand and move it around and around his palm. When you come to the words "up into his house," slowly crawl up your child's arm, and on the word "house," tickle him under the chin.

> *Where do you think the birdie lives?*
> *Where do you think the birdie lives?*
> *'Round and 'round and*
> *'Round and 'round and*
> *Up into his house.*

◆ Switch parts and let your child play the game on your hand.

What your two year old will learn:
FUN

Measure the Sunflowers

◆ Sunflowers often grow as high as ten feet, at a rate of about six inches a week.

◆ Put a wall chart next to your child's height chart.

◆ Plant sunflower seeds and carefully water them as needed.

◆ Once a week, measure the growth and show your child where the height is on the wall chart. Compare it to your child's height.

◆ Let your child make a mark or draw something on the chart at the height of the Sunflower. In a few weeks, he will begin to understand that the flower is actually growing.

◆ Compare the growth to his growth.

◆ This game helps children understand what it means to grow. It also develops their understanding of counting.

What your two year old will learn:
ABOUT GROWING

Spring Is Coming

◆ The first signs of spring are always exciting. To see a blade of grass peeping through the ground or hear a bird chirping always reminds us of the wonder of nature.

◆ Walk outside with your two year old and look at all the signs of spring.

◆ Recite the following poem:

> *Spring is coming, spring is coming,*
> *How do you think I know?*
> *I see a flower budding,*
> *I know it must be so.*
>
> *Spring is coming, spring is coming,*
> *How do you think I know?*
> *I see a blossom on the tree,*
> *I know it must be so.*

◆ Continue reciting the poem and add your own verses with signs of spring that you observe.

What your two year old will learn:
OBSERVATION SKILLS

The Surprise

◆ Read books about caterpillars and look for pictures in magazines as well.

◆ Look for pictures of butterflies in books and magazines.

◆ Search outdoors for caterpillars and for butterflies.

◆ Recite the following poem and perform the actions:

> *"Let's go to sleep," the caterpillars said,*
> *(bend all ten fingers into your palm)*
> *And they tucked themselves into their beds.*
> *They will awaken by and by,*
> *(slowly unfold each finger at a time)*
> *And each one will be a butterfly.*
> *(fly with your arms)*

◆ What your two year old will learn:
OBSERVATION SKILLS

Hot Summer Fun

◆ Go outside in a bathing suit or clothing that it is okay to get wet.

◆ Turn on a sprinkler and play games with it. A sprinkler that turns in a circle is preferred.

◆ Explain to your two year old how the water moves in a circle. Help him to anticipate when the water is coming.

◆ Start by putting an arm or a leg in the water when it comes to you. Keep adding more parts of the body.

◆ Another sprinkler game is chasing the water as the sprinkler turns.

◆ Play a game with a hose. Turn it on so that the water is a soft and gentle stream.

◆ Let your child fill containers, wash the trees, get you wet, make designs in the air and have fun.

◆ What your two year old will learn:
FUN

Rocks

◆ Looking for rocks is a wonderful way to satisfy your two year old's natural curiosity.

◆ Find a box for rock collecting. A shoe box works very well.

◆ Go on a rock hunt. Your child will love finding rocks and putting them into the box.

◆ When you return home, there are several games that you can play with the rocks.

◆ First, wash the rocks. Give your child a pan of water and a sponge, and he will be thrilled. Lay them on paper towels to dry.

◆ Pick up each rock and talk about how it feels. Is it smooth? Is it bumpy?

◆ Sort the rocks in different ways: by size, by color, by shape or by texture.

◆ Your child will treasure the rocks for a long time and enjoy them over and over.

 What your two year old will learn:
ABOUT NATURE PLAYING

Rain Songs

◆ Get dressed in your rain clothes, go outside and sing or recite rain songs and poems.

It's raining, it's pouring,
The old man is snoring.
He went to bed and bumped his head,
And he didn't get up until morning.

◆ ◆ ◆ ◆ ◆ ◆ ◆ ◆ ◆ ◆ ◆ ◆ ◆

Slip on your raincoat,
Put on your galoshes,
Wading in the puddles
Makes splishes and sploshes.

◆ ◆ ◆ ◆ ◆ ◆ ◆ ◆ ◆ ◆ ◆ ◆ ◆

Rain, rain, go away,
Come again another day.
Little _____ (child's name) wants to play,
Rain, rain, go away.

◆ ◆ ◆ ◆ ◆ ◆ ◆ ◆ ◆ ◆ ◆ ◆ ◆

Rain, rain, falling on the ground,
Pitter, patter, what a lovely sound.
Rain, rain, falling on my nose,
Drip, drip, drip, drip,
Squooshing in my toes.

◆ ◆ ◆ ◆ ◆ ◆ ◆ ◆ ◆ ◆ ◆ ◆ ◆

Dr. Foster went to Gloucester
In a shower of rain.
He stepped in a puddle
Right up to his middle
And never went there again.

What your two year old will learn:
ABOUT NATURE

Fascinating Bugs

◆ Show your two year old pictures cut from magazines of bugs. Flies, bees and spiders will be familiar to her.

◆ Go out into the yard and section off a small area by drawing in the dirt with a stick.

◆ Look closely to see if anything is moving within that area.

◆ Find a magnifying glass and let your child look for bugs with it.

◆ You will be amazed at what you see.

◆ Take the magnifying glass to another part of the yard and repeat the game.

What your two year old will learn:

OBSERVATION SKILLS

The Sun Is in the Sky

◆ Walk outside with your two year old and talk about all the things that you see. The sun, the trees, the grass and more.

◆ Sing to the tune of "The Farmer in the Dell":

> *The sun is in the sky,*
> *The sun is in the sky,*
> *Hi, ho, the derry oh,*
> *The sun is in the sky.*

◆ Ask your child where the grass is.

> *The grass is on the ground,*
> *The grass is on the ground,*
> *Hi, ho, the derry oh,*
> *The grass is on the ground.*

◆ Keep asking questions and make up a verse to sing about each answer.

> *The sky is very blue.... (teaching colors)*
> *The grass is very green.... (teaching colors)*
> *The sun feels very warm.... (sensory awareness)*
> *The bugs crawl on the ground.... (spatial awareness)*

 What your two year old will learn:
OBSERVATION SKILLS

What's in the Box?

This is a wonderful thinking game

◆ Go outside with your two year old and collect familiar objects: leaves, rocks, acorns, a flower, etc.

◆ Lay each of the objects on the ground and talk about them. Say their names and something about them, for example, "The leaves are on the trees."

◆ Take three items and put them into a box which you have brought with you outdoors. A shoe box works well.

◆ As you place articles in the box, repeat their names. You might let your two year old put them in the box.

◆ Tell your child to cover his eyes as you say the following poem:

> *Open the door, open the locks,*
> *I will take something out of the box.*

◆ Remove one item and put it with the others outside of the box. See if your child can tell you what is missing from the box.

◆ As your two year old plays this game, you can put more things into the box. You can even remove two items at a time.

 What your two year old will learn:
OBSERVATION SKILLS

Caterpillar

◆ Look at magazines or books with pictures of caterpillars and butterflies. A good book to read is *The Very Hungry Caterpillar* by Eric Carle.

◆ Talk about how caterpillars go to sleep and then wake up as butterflies.

◆ Say the following rhyme with your child and perform the actions:

A caterpillar crawled to the top of the tree,
   (crawl your fingers up your child's arm)
"I think I'll take a nap," says he.
   (rest your hand in a fist under your child's neck)
So under a leaf he began to creep
To spin his cocoon,
And he fell asleep.

All winter long he slept in his bed,
Till spring came along one day and said,
"Wake up, wake up, you sleepyhead,
Wake up, it's time to get out of bed."
So he opened his eyes on that sunny day,
   (make a butterfly by hooking your thumbs together)
He was a butterfly and flew away.
   (make your hands fly away)

What your two year old will learn:
ABOUT NATURE

Outside Creatures

◆ Take your two year old on a walk outdoors. Look for animals and insects.

◆ When you see a squirrel or a chipmunk, talk about how they move. Try to imitate their movements.

◆ Look for clues that an animal has been around. Holes in the ground and footprints in the dirt are good signs.

◆ Listen to the sounds of the birds and see whether you can figure out from the sounds where they are singing.

◆ Look for bird nests and squirrel nests in the trees.

◆ Sit together and feel the air on your faces and smell the wonderful aromas of the outdoors.

 What your two year old will learn:
ABOUT NATURE

Little Flower

◆ Plant seeds in two pots. Put one pot in full sun and give the other no sun at all.

◆ Water the pots each day.

◆ Your child will begin to understand how important sunshine is for growth.

◆ Repeat the experiment, but place both pots in full sun. Only water one of them. Again, your two year old will see dramatically how important water is for growth.

◆ Look at the flowers outside and talk about how once they were tiny seeds, and now they are beautiful flowers.

◆ Recite the following poem and perform the actions:

Little flower in the ground, (stoop down to the ground)
Now it is spring, and I have found (look all around)
The earth is warm, (look down to the earth)
The sky is blue, (look up to the sky)
*Come and stretch your arms so new, (stand up and
    stretch out your arms)*
Oh, pretty flower, I love you. (give your child a big hug)

 What your two year old will learn:
ABOUT GROWING

A Growing Seed

◆ After your child has experienced planting seeds and watching them grow, this fingerplay offers a nice reinforcement.

Once there was a seed in the dark, dark, ground.
  (hide one finger in the fist of your other hand)
Out came the sun so big and round,
  (make a circle with your arms)
Down came the rain so gentle and slow,
  (wiggle your fingers for the rain)
Up came the little seed, grow, grow, grow.
  (push your finger through your closed fist)

 What your two year old will learn:
COORDINATION

Starlight

◆ Take a blanket outside on a summer evening, lie down and look at the sky.

◆ Talk about the moon, the stars, the planets, airplanes, birds, etc.

◆ Your two year old will adore looking at the sky. Help her to imagine the astronauts on the moon.

◆ Explain what the word "wish" means and teach her to wish on the first star.

> *Starlight, star bright,*
> *First star I see tonight,*
> *I wish I may, I wish I might,*
> *Have this wish I wish tonight.*

◆ This is also the perfect time to sing "Twinkle, Twinkle, Little Star."

> *Twinkle, twinkle, little star,*
> *How I wonder what you are.*
> *Up above the earth so high,*
> *Like a diamond in the sky,*
> *Twinkle, twinkle, little star,*
> *How I wonder what you are.*

 What your two year old will learn:
ABOUT THE NIGHT SKY

Quiet Games

The Surprise Bag

◆ Fill a shopping bag with three or four familiar objects that your child will recognize.

◆ Sit on the floor with your two year old facing you.

◆ Very dramatically and very slowly, pull one object out of the shopping bag.

◆ As you take out the object, ask your child, "Do you know what I am taking out of the bag?"

◆ Give the object to your child to hold as you talk about its name, its color, how it feels and what it is used for.

◆ Ask your child to put the object back into the bag.

◆ Repeat this activity with another object.

◆ This is a nice poem to recite before taking each object out of the bag.

> *Mickety, mackety, mockety mag,*
> *What do I have inside of my bag?*

◆ Objects that you could have in the bag include a crayon, a toy car, silverware, a drinking cup, etc.

 What your two year old will learn:
LANGUAGE SKILLS

Touch Your Nose

◆ This is a nice fingerplay for a quiet time when you and your two year old are together.

◆ Ask her to touch her nose, her chin, her eyes, her knees, her hair, her ear and her elbows.

◆ Say the poem and act it out.

> *Touch your nose,*
> *Touch your chin,*
> *That is how the game begins.*
> *Touch your eyes,*
> *Touch your knees,*
> *Now pretend you're going to sneeze.*
> *Touch your hair,*
> *Touch your ear,*
> *Touch your sweet lips right here.*
> *Touch your elbows,*
> *Make them bend,*
> *Now this little game will end.*

 What your two year old will learn:
LISTENING SKILLS

The Clock Game

◆ Recite the nursery rhyme "Hickory, Dickory, Dock" with your child.

◆ Tell your child that the clock says, "tick, tock."

◆ Walk around the room stiffly with your arms to your sides, saying, "tick, tock, tick, tock."

◆ Tell your child that the clock is going to hide and see whether she can find it.

◆ It is okay if your child watches where you hide.

◆ Now say, "Can you find the clock? Tick, tock, tick, tock."

◆ When your child finds you, praise her for the good job she has done.

◆ After you have played this game for awhile, your child will want to be the clock.

 What your two year old will learn:
LISTENING SKILLS

Listening Game

◆ Pick three objects with which your two year old is familiar, for example, a whistle, a rattle, a toy that makes noise or an alarm clock.

◆ Talk about each object and the sound that it makes.

◆ Show your child one of the objects. Ask him to close his eyes and listen to the sound.

◆ Put the object down. Ask him to open his eyes and give you the thing that was making the noise.

◆ Repeat this with each article until you are sure that your two year old knows what each one sounds like.

◆ Now you can play the game. Ask your child to close his eyes and listen to the sound that you make.

◆ See if he can tell you which object makes the sound.

 What your two year old will learn:
LISTENING SKILLS

Apple Fun

◆ Two year olds are beginning to identify colors. The first step is to be able to match colors.

◆ Fill a sack with both red and green apples.

◆ Let your child take the apples out of the sack one at a time.

◆ Each time he takes an apple out of the sack, say, "Oh, boy, a green apple" or "Oh, boy, a red apple."

◆ When all the apples are out of the sack (no more than six or eight), sort them into two piles by color.

◆ Ask your child to put all the red ones back into the sack and then to put all of the green ones back into the sack.

◆ After you have played this game a few times, your child will begin to understand how to separate the apples by color.

 What your two year old will learn:
MATCHING SKILLS

Water Games

◆ There is something very satisfying about playing with water, and two year olds have a great attraction to water. Here are some water games that they will enjoy.

Wiping tabletops and countertops with a sponge.
Spraying water with a spray bottle on objects and wiping them dry.
Washing dishes and putting them into another container for rinsing.
Pouring water from one container to another.
   (This is a great bathtub game.)
Filling a baster with water and squishing it out.
Floating water toys in the bathtub.
Experimenting with what sinks or floats in a bathtub.

What your two year old will learn:
COORDINATION

Dropsies

◆ You will need two cardboard tubes of equal length but different diameter. Wrapping paper tubes and paper towel tubes are good.

◆ Select some of your child's toys that will fit into the tubes.

◆ Let your child choose a toy. Tell her into which tube to put the toy. Show her how to hold the tube at an angle so that the toy will fall out the other side.

◆ When the toy has been retrieved, play the game again.

◆ After you have done this a few times, let your two year old decide into which tube the toy should go. Whichever one she selects, always say, "You chose the big tube" or "You chose the little tube."

◆ It is fun to say something as you put the toy into the tube. Words like "shazam" or "taa daa" make the game more interesting.

◆ This game has other benefits. It stimulates tracking, which is the ability to follow a moving object with the eyes, and it helps children understand the concepts of big and little.

 What your two year old will learn:
THE CONCEPTS OF BIG & LITTLE

Boxing Practice

◆ Find three boxes of different sizes with separate lids. Shoe boxes are good for this activity.

◆ Decorate each box and its lid with stickers, making sure that the stickers on the box and the lid match.

◆ Show the boxes to your child with the lids on.

◆ Ask your two year old to take off the lids.

◆ Now ask him to put the lids back on again.

◆ He will probably try to put a lid on a box that it does not fit. When he discovers the correct box, praise him highly.

◆ Talk about the stickers on the boxes. Show him that the tops and bottoms have the same stickers.

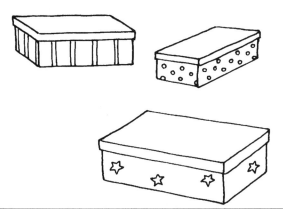

 What your two year old will learn:
MATCHING SKILLS

The Sorting Game

◆ Chances are that your two year old has many toys strewn all over the place.

◆ This game helps clean up the toys and teaches matching skills at the same time.

◆ Pick one category, for example, blocks, and go on a search all over the house. Your child will enjoy this very much. Make it fun by saying things like, "block, block, where are you?" "Oh, here you are!"

◆ Put all of the blocks into a container.

◆ Try matching the blocks by size. Pick one block and ask your child to find another of the same size.

◆ You can also match blocks by color.

◆ When you have finished with blocks, start looking for other categories. Cars and dolls are good.

 What your two year old will learn:
MATCHING SKILLS

Bump Dity Bump

◆ Take your index finger and tap it gently on your child's nose as you say the following:

> *Take your finger and go like this,*
> *Bump dity, bump dity, bump, bump, bump.*
> *Take your finger and go like this,*
> *Bump dity, bump dity, bump, bump, bump,*
> *Bump dity, bump dity, bump, bump, bump,*
> *Bump dity, bump dity, bump, bump, bump.*
> *Take your finger and go like this,*
> *Bump dity, bump dity, bump, bump, bump.*

◆ Take your child's index finger and help him "bump dity" on your nose.

◆ You can "bump dity" on different parts of the body—your head, your knees, etc.

◆ Your child will love this game and want to play it over and over.

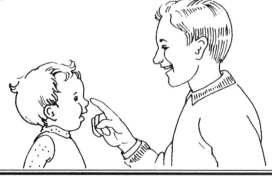

 What your two year old will learn:
BODY AWARENESS

My Hands

◆ Draw outlines of your hand and of your child's hand on a piece of heavy white paper.

◆ Point out to your child that your hand is larger than his hand.

◆ Let your child color the hands, using large crayons.

◆ Cut out the shapes and glue them onto a larger piece of paper for hanging on the wall.

◆ Talk about all the different things that you can do with your hands.

◆ Ask your child to do many things with his hands.

> *Shake hands.*
> *Wave goodbye.*
> *Wave hello.*
> *Wiggle his fingers.*
> *Put his fingers to his lips for "shhh."*
> *Hold his hand out for "stop."*

What your two year old will learn:
BODY AWARENESS

'Round and 'Round

◆ Show your child how to make a fist with her hand and roll one hand over the other.

◆ Say the following rhyme and perform the actions:

> *'Round and 'round and 'round and 'round and*
> *Up, up, up. (put hands up high in the air)*
> *'Round and 'round and 'round and 'round and*
> *Down, down, down. (put hands down)*
> *'Round and 'round and 'round and 'round and*
> *Out, out, out. (roll hands away from you)*
> *'Round and 'round and 'round and 'round and*
> *In, in, in. (bring hands toward you)*

 What your two year old will learn:
SPATIAL CONCEPTS

A Hunting We Will Go

◆ Sit on the floor holding your child in your arms.

◆ Recite the following poem:

> *A hunting we will go,*
> *A hunting we will go,*
> *We'll catch a fox and put him in a box,*
> *And then we'll let him go.*

◆ On the last line, open your arms and let your child go.

◆ Show your child how to hide behind a chair. On the words "A hunting we will go," pretend to be looking for him.

◆ On the words "We'll catch a fox," pretend to catch him. On the last line, open your arms and let him go.

What your two year old will learn:
FUN

Would You Please?

◆ My two year old nephew adores this game and feels a great sense of accomplishment when he is able to follow the directions.

◆ Starting with the words "Would you please," ask your child to perform a task. For example: "Would you please give me your teddy bear?"

◆ Once your child can understand what you have asked, continue to make each direction a little harder. You will see the little wheels turning in his head as he thinks about what he has to do.

◆ Always start each direction with the words "Would you please?" Doing this will tell your child that you want to play the game. In fact, he will probably come to you and ask to play the game.

◆ Here are a few "Would you please?" questions.

Would you please bring me my hat?
Would you please go to Daddy's room and bring me my shoes?
Would you please go to the bathroom and bring me some soap?
Would you please open the drawer and give me a spoon?

 What your two year old will learn:
LISTENING SKILLS

Getting Into Shapes

◆ You will need blocks of different shapes to play this game. Circles, squares and triangles are good to start with.

◆ Give your child the circular block and let him hold it and feel its shape. Talk about its name and point out other circles in the room.

◆ Give your child another block of a different shape. Talk about this shape.

◆ Take the first and second blocks and place them into a sack or large bag.

◆ Hold another circular block in your hand. Show it to him and ask him to find the matching shape in the sack.

◆ At first, he can put his hand into the sack and look at what he takes out. As he gets better at the game, encourage him to identify the shape by feeling the block.

◆ As he puts his hand into the sack, sing this song to the tune of "London Bridge Is Falling Down."

Find the block that looks like this,
Looks like this, looks like this,
Find the block that looks like this,
Can you find it?

 What your two year old will learn:
MATCHING SKILLS

Blow the Wind

◆ Sit your two year old in your lap and show her how to blow gently with her lips.

◆ Blow gently on her hand and ask her to blow gently on your hand.

◆ Recite this poem to your child.

> *I can blow like the wind. (blow gently)*
> *I can bring the rain. (move your fingers up and down*
>   *her arm)*
> *When I blow very softly,*
> *I can whisper your name. (whisper your child's name)*

◆ Whispering is difficult for a two year old. It takes concentration and good listening skills. She will enjoy practicing with this poem.

 What your two year old will learn:
BONDING

Here Sits the Lord Mayor

◆ This is a very sweet game to play with your two year old.

◆ Sit your child on your lap and say the following:

> *Here sits the Lord Mayor. (tap your finger on top of*
> *your child's head)*
> *Here sit his men. (gently touch your child's eyes)*
> *Here sits the cock, (tap one cheek)*
> *And here sits the hen. (tap the other cheek)*
> *Here sit the little chickens. (touch your child's mouth)*
> *Here they run in. (tap your fingers on your child's lips)*
> *Chin chopper, chin chopper,*
> *Chin chopper, chin. (tap your child's chin)*

 What your two year old will learn:
FUN

It's in the Cards

◆ Playing cards is a terrific game for a two year old.

◆ Looking at the cards, dropping them on the ground and picking them up again will keep your child occupied for a long time.

◆ Play a pretend game of cards with your child.

◆ Deal out about ten cards, saying, "One for you and one for me." When all the cards are dealt, turn them over and talk about the pictures.

◆ Cut a slit in the top of a shoe box. Give your child a card to drop through the slit.

◆ Pretend you are mailing letters: "Here, mail this letter to Uncle Jim."

◆ What your two year old will learn:
HAND-EYE COORDINATION

Who's in the Picture?

◆ With your child along, take pictures of familiar places: your house, your yard, etc. Be sure and let your child be in a lot of the pictures.

◆ Develop two copies of the pictures.

◆ Look through the pictures with your two year old and talk about each one. He will be delighted when he sees himself in the pictures.

◆ Pick out three pictures and place them in a pile.

◆ Give your child a picture that matches one of the three, and ask him to find the matching picture in the pile.

◆ When he matches the picture, praise him generously.

◆ Keep adding new pictures.

◆ Put the pictures in ziplock bags, and your child will have his own photo collection.

 What your two year old will learn:
MATCHING SKILLS

Hop a Little

◆ This poem has a lot of directions. It works best if you practice each line and the actions several times.

◆ Once you have gone over all the words a few times, recite it as a poem.

Hop a little, jump a little,
One, two, three.
Run a little, skip a little,
Tap one knee.
Bend a little, stretch a little,
Nod your head.
Yawn a little, sleep a little,
In your bed.
Good night.

 What your two year old will learn:
TO FOLLOW DIRECTIONS

Here is the Church

◆ Recite the fingerplay and carry out the actions. This takes practice, and your child will feel a great sense of accomplishment when she succeeds.

Here is the church, (join your hands together and interlock your fingers with the fingers downward)
Here is the steeple, (lift the two index fingers to form the steeple)
Open the doors, (turn your interlocked hands palms upward)
And see all the people. (wiggle your fingers)

What your two year old will learn:
COORDINATION

Index

Games to Play with Babies
Revised and Expanded

Jackie Silberg

Here are 250 fun-filled games to help babies (from birth to twelve months) explore their world and learn critical developmental skills. Language, coordination and problem-solving are some of the areas covered. But the important value is fun. Both adult and baby will have hours of enjoyable time together. This book works for both parents and caregivers. 286 pages.

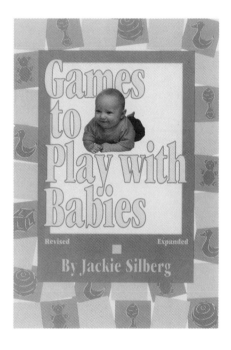

ISBN 0-87659-162-4   **Gryphon House**
11144   **Paperback**

Games to Play with Toddlers

Jackie Silberg

Toddlers (twelve to twenty-four months) love to explore. The games in this practical book will help one to two year olds learn language and expand their creativity, observation and coordination skills. They will get practice in problem-solving, following directions and more. Another book for both caregivers and parents. 285 pages.

ISBN 0-87659-163-2   **Gryphon House**
16264   **Paperback**

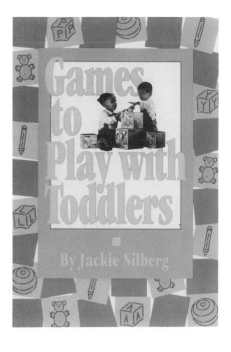

Where is Thumbkin?

500 Activities to Use with Songs
You Already Know

Pam Schiller, Thomas Moore

Connect learning across the curriculum
- using familiar songs! Enjoy activities that
relate to every learning center - science, art,
language, math, motor skills, drama, social
studies, cooking. 256 pages

ISBN 0-87659-164-0   **Gryphon House**
13156   **Paperback**

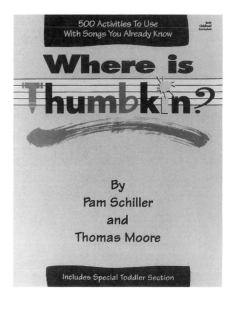

The GIANT Encyclopedia of Theme Activities For Children 2 to 5:

Over 600 Favorite Activities
Created by Teachers for Teachers

The result of a nationwide competition, this exciting book covers 48 themes - with teacher-developed Activities to enthrall and delight children as they learn. 512 pages.

ISBN 0-87659-166-7   **Gryphon House**
19216   **Paperback**